62 Brunch and Tea Recipes for Home

By: Kelly Johnson

Table of Contents

Brunch Recipes

- Avocado Toast with Poached Eggs
- Baked French Toast Casserole
- Smoked Salmon Bagels
- Eggs Benedict
- Fruit Parfait
- Blueberry Pancakes
- Quiche Lorraine
- Greek Yogurt and Berry Smoothie Bowl
- Shakshuka
- Banana Walnut Muffins
- Spinach and Feta Breakfast Wraps
- Cinnamon Roll Waffles
- Sausage and Mushroom Strata
- Lemon Ricotta Pancakes
- Vegetarian Breakfast Burritos
- Breakfast Pizza
- Caprese Avocado Toast
- Sweet Potato Hash
- Pesto and Tomato Bruschetta
- Chia Seed Pudding
- Ham and Cheese Croissants
- Coconut Pancakes
- Egg and Bacon Breakfast Quesadillas

- Chocolate Banana Bread
- Prosciutto-Wrapped Asparagus
- Ricotta and Berry Stuffed Crepes
- Breakfast Tacos
- Sourdough Breakfast Sandwich
- Carmelized Onion and Goat Cheese Frittata
- Peaches and Cream Stuffed French Toast
- Bacon and egg Breakfast Pies

Tea Recipes
- Classic Black Tea
- Green Tea with Mint
- Chai Latte
- Iced Lemon Tea
- Earl Grey Tea Latte
- Hibiscus Herbal Tea
- Jasmine Pearl Tea
- Masala Chai
- Peach Ginger White Tea
- Mango Black Tea Punch
- Turmeric Ginger Tea
- Rose Milk Tea
- Matcha Latte
- Spiced Apple Chai
- Lavender Chamomile Tea
- Pomegranate White Tea Spritzer
- Cinnamon Orange Rooibos Tea

- Coconut Almond Chai
- Blueberry Mint Iced Tea
- Ginger Turmeric Golden Milk Tea
- CHocolate Chai Latte
- Minty Moroccan Mint Tea
- Lemon Lavender Black Tea
- Cranberry Orange Spice Tea
- Vanilla Rooibos Latte
- Strawberry Basil Iced Tea
- Chamomile Honey GInger Tea
- Pumpkin Spice Chai
- Blackberry Sage Tea
- Coconut Chai Iced Tea
- Raspberry Rosehip Herbal Tea

Brunch:

Avocado Toast with Poached Eggs

Ingredients:

- 2 slices of your favorite bread (sourdough or whole grain work well)
- 1 ripe avocado
- 2 large eggs
- Salt and pepper to taste
- Optional toppings: red pepper flakes, cherry tomatoes, feta cheese, cilantro, or hot sauce

Instructions:

Toast the Bread:

- Toast the bread slices to your desired level of crispiness.

Prepare the Avocado:

- While the bread is toasting, cut the ripe avocado in half and remove the pit. Scoop out the avocado flesh into a bowl.

Mash the Avocado:

- Mash the avocado with a fork until you achieve your desired consistency. Some people prefer a smooth spread, while others like it a bit chunky.

Season the Avocado:

- Add salt and pepper to taste. You can also add a squeeze of lemon juice for some acidity and extra flavor.

Poach the Eggs:

- Bring a pot of water to a gentle simmer. Add a splash of white vinegar to the water; this helps the egg whites coagulate more easily.
- Crack one egg into a small bowl. Create a gentle whirlpool in the simmering water with a spoon and carefully slide the egg into the center of the whirlpool.
- Poach the egg for about 3-4 minutes for a runny yolk, or longer if you prefer a firmer yolk.
- Repeat the process for the second egg.

Assemble the Avocado Toast:

- Spread the mashed avocado evenly over the toasted bread slices.

Top with Poached Eggs:

- Carefully lift the poached eggs out of the water with a slotted spoon, allowing any excess water to drain off. Place one poached egg on each slice of avocado toast.

Season Again (Optional):

- Sprinkle a bit more salt and pepper on top of the poached eggs. You can also add any optional toppings like red pepper flakes, cherry tomatoes, feta cheese, cilantro, or hot sauce.

Serve Immediately:

- Avocado toast with poached eggs is best enjoyed immediately while the eggs are still warm and the toast is crispy.

Feel free to customize the recipe based on your preferences, and enjoy this nutritious and satisfying breakfast or brunch option!

Baked French Toast Casserole

Ingredients:

For the Casserole:

- 1 loaf of French bread, preferably a day or two old, cut into 1-inch cubes
- 8 large eggs
- 2 cups whole milk
- 1/2 cup heavy cream
- 1/2 cup granulated sugar
- 1/2 cup brown sugar, packed
- 1 tablespoon vanilla extract
- 1/2 teaspoon ground cinnamon
- 1/4 teaspoon salt

For the Topping:

- 1/2 cup all-purpose flour
- 1/2 cup brown sugar, packed
- 1 teaspoon ground cinnamon
- 1/4 teaspoon salt
- 1/2 cup cold unsalted butter, cut into small cubes

Optional toppings:

- Maple syrup
- Powdered sugar
- Fresh berries

- Chopped nuts

Instructions:

Prepare the Bread:
- Cut the French bread into 1-inch cubes. If the bread is fresh, you can let it sit out for a few hours or overnight to slightly dry it out.

Make the Egg Mixture:
- In a large mixing bowl, whisk together the eggs, whole milk, heavy cream, granulated sugar, brown sugar, vanilla extract, ground cinnamon, and salt.

Assemble the Casserole:
- Grease a 9x13-inch baking dish and spread the cubed bread evenly in the dish.
- Pour the egg mixture over the bread, ensuring that all the bread is coated. Press down on the bread with a spatula to help it absorb the liquid.

Prepare the Topping:
- In a separate bowl, mix together the flour, brown sugar, ground cinnamon, and salt.
- Add the cold, cubed butter and use a pastry cutter or your fingers to combine until the mixture resembles coarse crumbs.

Add the Topping:
- Sprinkle the topping evenly over the bread mixture in the baking dish.

Chill (Optional):
- At this point, you can cover the casserole with plastic wrap and refrigerate it overnight, allowing the flavors to meld and the bread to fully absorb the liquid.

Bake:

- Preheat the oven to 350°F (175°C).
- If you refrigerated the casserole, let it come to room temperature before baking.
- Bake for 45-55 minutes or until the top is golden brown and the center is set.

Serve:

- Let the casserole rest for a few minutes before serving.
- Cut into squares and serve with optional toppings such as maple syrup, powdered sugar, fresh berries, or chopped nuts.

This baked French toast casserole is a delightful and comforting breakfast treat that's sure to please a crowd. Enjoy!

Smoked Salmon Bagels

Ingredients:

- 4 bagels (your choice of flavor)
- 8 oz (about 225g) smoked salmon
- 1/2 cup cream cheese, softened
- 1 tablespoon capers, drained
- 1 small red onion, thinly sliced
- Fresh dill, chopped (for garnish)
- Lemon wedges (for serving)

Instructions:

Prepare the Bagels:
- Slice the bagels in half and toast them to your liking.

Spread Cream Cheese:
- Spread a generous layer of softened cream cheese on each half of the bagels.

Add Smoked Salmon:
- Lay slices of smoked salmon evenly on top of the cream cheese.

Top with Red Onion and Capers:
- Scatter thinly sliced red onion and capers over the smoked salmon. These ingredients add a burst of flavor and a bit of tanginess to the dish.

Garnish with Fresh Dill:
- Sprinkle fresh dill over the top for a touch of herbaceous freshness.

Serve with Lemon Wedges:

- Serve the smoked salmon bagels with lemon wedges on the side. Squeezing fresh lemon juice over the salmon adds brightness to the dish.

Optional Additions:

- You can customize your smoked salmon bagels by adding extras like sliced tomatoes, cucumber, or avocado for added freshness.

Serve and Enjoy:

- Arrange the prepared bagels on a serving platter and enjoy them as a delicious and satisfying meal.

Smoked salmon bagels are not only tasty but also versatile, allowing you to add your favorite toppings to suit your preferences. Whether you're serving them for brunch or as a quick and indulgent breakfast, they are sure to be a hit!

Eggs Benedict

Ingredients:

For the Hollandaise Sauce:

- 3 large egg yolks
- 1 tablespoon lemon juice
- 1/2 cup unsalted butter, melted
- Pinch of cayenne pepper
- Salt, to taste

For the Eggs Benedict:

- 4 English muffins, split and toasted

- 8 slices Canadian bacon or ham
- 8 large eggs
- Salt and pepper, to taste
- Chopped chives or parsley, for garnish (optional)

Instructions:

Prepare the Hollandaise Sauce:
- In a heatproof bowl, whisk together the egg yolks and lemon juice until well combined.

Double Boiler Method for Hollandaise:
- Place the bowl over a pot of simmering water (double boiler) but ensure that the bottom of the bowl does not touch the water.

Whisk and Cook:
- Continue whisking the egg yolk mixture while gradually drizzling in the melted butter. Whisk until the sauce thickens to a creamy consistency.
- Add a pinch of cayenne pepper and salt to taste. Remove the bowl from the heat and set aside.

Poach the Eggs:
- Bring a pot of water to a gentle simmer. Add a splash of white vinegar to help the egg whites coagulate more easily.
- Crack one egg into a small bowl. Create a gentle whirlpool in the simmering water with a spoon and carefully slide the egg into the center of the whirlpool.
- Poach the egg for about 3-4 minutes for a runny yolk or longer if you prefer a firmer yolk.

- Repeat the process for the remaining eggs.

Assemble the Eggs Benedict:

- While the eggs are poaching, toast the English muffin halves and warm the Canadian bacon or ham slices.

Layering:

- Place a slice of Canadian bacon or ham on each toasted English muffin half.
- Carefully place a poached egg on top of the bacon or ham.

Hollandaise Sauce:

- Spoon a generous amount of hollandaise sauce over each poached egg.

Garnish and Serve:

- Optionally, garnish with chopped chives or parsley for added freshness.

Serve Immediately:

- Serve the Eggs Benedict immediately while the eggs and hollandaise sauce are warm.

Eggs Benedict is a classic and elegant brunch option that's sure to impress. Enjoy this delicious dish with your favorite breakfast beverage!

Fruit Parfait

Ingredients:

- 1 cup Greek yogurt (or your favorite yogurt)
- 2 tablespoons honey or maple syrup (for sweetening the yogurt)
- 1 teaspoon vanilla extract
- 1 cup granola (homemade or store-bought)
- 1 cup mixed fresh fruits (berries, sliced bananas, kiwi, mango, etc.)
- 1/4 cup nuts (such as almonds or walnuts), chopped (optional)
- Fresh mint leaves for garnish (optional)

Instructions:

Prepare the Yogurt:
- In a bowl, mix the Greek yogurt with honey or maple syrup and vanilla extract. Adjust the sweetness to your liking.

Layering:
- In serving glasses or bowls, start by adding a layer of the sweetened yogurt at the bottom.

Add Granola:
- Sprinkle a layer of granola over the yogurt. This adds a delicious crunch to the parfait.

Layer with Fruits:
- Add a layer of mixed fresh fruits on top of the granola. You can use a variety of fruits for a colorful and flavorful parfait.

Repeat Layers:

- Repeat the layering process until you reach the top of the glass or bowl, finishing with a layer of yogurt.

Top with Fruits and Nuts:

- Garnish the top with additional fresh fruits and, if desired, chopped nuts for extra texture and flavor.

Garnish (Optional):

- Optionally, garnish the parfait with fresh mint leaves for a touch of freshness.

Serve Immediately:

- Serve the fruit parfait immediately for a delicious and refreshing treat.

Variations:

- Experiment with different flavors of yogurt, such as vanilla, strawberry, or coconut.
- Customize the parfait with your favorite fruits or seasonal fruits.
- Add a drizzle of honey or a sprinkle of cinnamon on top for extra sweetness and flavor.

Fruit parfaits are not only tasty but also a visually appealing and nutritious option. Enjoy this versatile dish for breakfast, as a snack, or a light dessert!

Blueberry Pancakes

Ingredients:

- 1 cup all-purpose flour
- 2 tablespoons sugar
- 1 teaspoon baking powder

- 1/2 teaspoon baking soda
- 1/4 teaspoon salt
- 3/4 cup buttermilk
- 1 large egg
- 2 tablespoons unsalted butter, melted
- 1 teaspoon vanilla extract
- 1 cup fresh or frozen blueberries
- Butter or oil for cooking

Instructions:

Prepare the Dry Ingredients:

- In a large bowl, whisk together the flour, sugar, baking powder, baking soda, and salt.

Prepare the Wet Ingredients:

- In a separate bowl, whisk together the buttermilk, egg, melted butter, and vanilla extract.

Combine Wet and Dry Ingredients:

- Pour the wet ingredients into the bowl with the dry ingredients. Gently fold the mixture until just combined. Be careful not to overmix; it's okay if there are a few lumps.

Add Blueberries:

- Gently fold in the blueberries into the batter. If using frozen blueberries, you can toss them in a little flour before adding to prevent them from sinking to the bottom.

Preheat the Griddle or Pan:

- Preheat a griddle or a non-stick skillet over medium heat. Add a small amount of butter or oil to grease the surface.

Cook the Pancakes:

- Pour 1/4 cup of batter onto the griddle for each pancake. Cook until bubbles form on the surface and the edges look set.

Flip and Cook:

- Flip the pancakes and cook for an additional 1-2 minutes on the other side, or until golden brown.

Repeat:

- Repeat the process with the remaining batter, adding more butter or oil to the griddle as needed.

Keep Warm:

- Keep the cooked pancakes warm in a low oven while you finish cooking the rest.

Serve:

- Serve the blueberry pancakes warm with maple syrup, additional blueberries, and a pat of butter if desired.

Feel free to customize these pancakes by adding a sprinkle of cinnamon or a dash of lemon zest to the batter for extra flavor. Enjoy your delicious blueberry pancakes for a delightful breakfast treat!

Quiche Lorraine

Ingredients:

For the Pie Crust:

- 1 1/4 cups all-purpose flour
- 1/2 cup unsalted butter, cold and cubed
- 1/4 teaspoon salt
- 3-4 tablespoons ice water

For the Filling:

- 8 ounces (about 225g) bacon, diced
- 1 cup shredded Gruyère or Swiss cheese
- 1 cup heavy cream
- 4 large eggs
- Salt and black pepper to taste
- Pinch of nutmeg (optional)

Instructions:

Prepare the Pie Crust:
- In a food processor, combine the flour, cold cubed butter, and salt. Pulse until the mixture resembles coarse crumbs.
- Add ice water, one tablespoon at a time, and pulse until the dough just comes together.
- Gather the dough, shape it into a disk, wrap it in plastic wrap, and refrigerate for at least 30 minutes.

Preheat the Oven:

- Preheat your oven to 375°F (190°C).

Roll Out the Dough:

- On a lightly floured surface, roll out the chilled dough to fit a 9-inch (23 cm) pie dish. Press the dough into the dish and trim the edges.

Pre-bake the Crust (Blind Baking):

- Line the pie crust with parchment paper and fill it with pie weights or dry beans. Bake for about 15 minutes.
- Remove the parchment paper and weights, then bake for an additional 5 minutes until the crust is lightly golden. Set aside.

Cook the Bacon:

- In a skillet, cook the diced bacon over medium heat until it becomes crispy. Remove excess grease by draining on paper towels.

Assemble the Filling:

- In a bowl, whisk together the heavy cream, eggs, salt, pepper, and nutmeg (if using).
- Spread the cooked bacon evenly over the pre-baked pie crust. Sprinkle shredded cheese on top.

Pour the Egg Mixture:

- Pour the egg and cream mixture over the bacon and cheese.

Bake:

- Bake in the preheated oven for 35-40 minutes or until the quiche is set and the top is golden brown.

Cool and Serve:

- Allow the Quiche Lorraine to cool for a few minutes before slicing. Serve warm or at room temperature.

Quiche Lorraine is versatile, and you can customize it by adding ingredients like sautéed onions, mushrooms, or spinach to suit your taste. Enjoy this classic French dish for brunch or a light dinner!

Greek Yogurt and Berry Smoothie Bowl

Ingredients:

For the Smoothie:

- 1 cup frozen mixed berries (strawberries, blueberries, raspberries)
- 1/2 cup Greek yogurt (plain or flavored)
- 1 ripe banana
- 1/2 cup almond milk (or your preferred milk)
- 1 tablespoon honey or maple syrup (optional, for sweetness)

For Toppings (Optional):

- Fresh berries (sliced strawberries, blueberries, raspberries)
- Granola
- Chia seeds
- Shredded coconut
- Nuts or seeds (almonds, walnuts, sunflower seeds)
- Drizzle of honey or maple syrup

Instructions:

Prepare the Smoothie:

- In a blender, combine the frozen mixed berries, Greek yogurt, ripe banana, almond milk, and honey or maple syrup if using.
- Blend until smooth and creamy. If the mixture is too thick, you can add more almond milk to achieve your desired consistency.

Assemble the Smoothie Bowl:

- Pour the smoothie into a bowl.

Add Toppings:

- Arrange your favorite toppings on top of the smoothie. This is where you can get creative and add a variety of textures and flavors.

Customize with Fresh Berries:

- Fresh berries not only add color but also freshness to the bowl. Feel free to mix and match based on what's in season.

Add Crunch with Granola:

- Sprinkle granola over the smoothie bowl for a satisfying crunch. You can use store-bought granola or make your own.

Include Texture with Chia Seeds:

- Chia seeds are a great source of fiber and add a delightful texture. Sprinkle them over the smoothie bowl.

Incorporate Nuts or Seeds:

- Add a handful of nuts or seeds for extra protein and crunch. Almonds, walnuts, or sunflower seeds work well.

Drizzle with Honey or Maple Syrup:

- If you prefer added sweetness, drizzle a bit of honey or maple syrup over the top.

Serve and Enjoy:

- Grab a spoon and enjoy your Greek Yogurt and Berry Smoothie Bowl!

Smoothie bowls are not only delicious but also a great way to pack in nutrients. Feel free to experiment with different combinations and make it your own!

Shakshuka

Ingredients:

- 2 tablespoons olive oil
- 1 onion, finely chopped
- 1 red bell pepper, diced
- 2 cloves garlic, minced
- 1 teaspoon ground cumin
- 1 teaspoon ground paprika
- 1/2 teaspoon ground coriander
- 1/4 teaspoon cayenne pepper (adjust to taste)
- Salt and black pepper, to taste
- 1 can (28 ounces) crushed tomatoes
- 4-6 large eggs
- Fresh parsley or cilantro, chopped (for garnish)
- Feta cheese or crumbled goat cheese (optional, for serving)
- Crusty bread or pita (for serving)

Instructions:

Sauté Vegetables:

- In a large skillet or pan, heat the olive oil over medium heat. Add chopped onions and diced red bell pepper. Sauté until the vegetables are softened, about 5-7 minutes.

Add Spices and Garlic:

- Stir in the minced garlic, ground cumin, ground paprika, ground coriander, cayenne pepper, salt, and black pepper. Cook for an additional 1-2 minutes until the spices become fragrant.

Pour in Crushed Tomatoes:

- Pour in the crushed tomatoes and stir well to combine. Allow the mixture to simmer for 10-15 minutes, allowing the flavors to meld and the sauce to thicken.

Make Wells for Eggs:

- Using the back of a spoon, make small wells in the tomato sauce. Crack each egg into a separate well, distributing them evenly across the skillet.

Poach the Eggs:

- Cover the skillet and let the eggs poach in the simmering tomato sauce for about 5-7 minutes or until the egg whites are set but the yolks are still runny.

Season and Garnish:

- Season the eggs with a pinch of salt and black pepper. Garnish with chopped fresh parsley or cilantro.

Optional Cheese:

- If desired, crumble feta cheese or goat cheese over the top for an extra layer of flavor.

Serve:

- Serve the Shakshuka directly from the skillet. Scoop out eggs along with the tomato sauce. It's traditionally served with crusty bread or pita for dipping.

Shakshuka is a versatile dish, and you can customize it by adding ingredients like spinach, feta, or olives. Enjoy this flavorful and hearty dish for a delicious breakfast or brunch!

Banana Walnut Muffins

Ingredients:

- 2 to 3 ripe bananas, mashed
- 1/2 cup unsalted butter, melted
- 1 teaspoon vanilla extract
- 1/2 cup granulated sugar
- 1/4 cup brown sugar, packed
- 1 large egg
- 1 1/2 cups all-purpose flour
- 1 teaspoon baking soda
- 1/2 teaspoon baking powder
- 1/2 teaspoon ground cinnamon
- 1/4 teaspoon salt
- 1/2 cup chopped walnuts (plus extra for topping, if desired)

Instructions:

Preheat the Oven:

- Preheat your oven to 350°F (175°C). Line a muffin tin with paper liners or grease the cups.

Mash the Bananas:

- In a large bowl, mash the ripe bananas with a fork or potato masher until mostly smooth.

Combine Wet Ingredients:

- Add melted butter, vanilla extract, granulated sugar, brown sugar, and the egg to the mashed bananas. Mix until well combined.

Combine Dry Ingredients:

- In a separate bowl, whisk together the flour, baking soda, baking powder, ground cinnamon, and salt.

Combine Wet and Dry Ingredients:

- Gradually add the dry ingredients to the banana mixture, stirring until just combined. Do not overmix.

Add Walnuts:

- Gently fold in the chopped walnuts into the batter.

Fill Muffin Cups:

- Spoon the batter into the prepared muffin cups, filling each about two-thirds full.

Optional: Add Walnut Topping:

- Optionally, sprinkle some extra chopped walnuts on top of each muffin for added texture.

Bake:

- Bake in the preheated oven for approximately 18-20 minutes, or until a toothpick inserted into the center of a muffin comes out clean or with a few moist crumbs.

Cool:

- Allow the muffins to cool in the tin for a few minutes before transferring them to a wire rack to cool completely.

Serve and Enjoy:

- Once cooled, serve the Banana Walnut Muffins and enjoy them with a cup of coffee or tea.

Feel free to customize these muffins by adding ingredients like chocolate chips, dried fruit, or a sprinkle of oats on top. These muffins are a great way to use up overripe bananas and make for a delicious and portable snack.

Spinach and Feta Breakfast Wraps

Ingredients:

- 4 large whole wheat or spinach-flavored tortillas
- 6 large eggs
- 1 cup fresh spinach, chopped
- 1/2 cup crumbled feta cheese
- 1 tablespoon olive oil
- Salt and pepper, to taste
- Optional toppings: diced tomatoes, avocado slices, hot sauce

Instructions:

Prepare Ingredients:
- Chop the fresh spinach, crumble the feta cheese, and have any optional toppings ready.

Scramble Eggs:
- In a bowl, whisk the eggs and season with salt and pepper.

Sauté Spinach:
- Heat olive oil in a pan over medium heat. Add the chopped spinach and sauté until wilted, about 1-2 minutes.

Add Eggs:
- Pour the whisked eggs into the pan with the sautéed spinach. Stir gently and cook until the eggs are scrambled and cooked through.

Add Feta:

- Add the crumbled feta cheese to the eggs and stir until the cheese is slightly melted and combined with the eggs and spinach.

Warm Tortillas:
- Warm the tortillas in a dry skillet or microwave for a few seconds to make them pliable.

Assemble Wraps:
- Divide the scrambled egg mixture evenly among the tortillas, placing it in the center.

Add Toppings:
- Add any optional toppings you desire, such as diced tomatoes or avocado slices.

Wrap and Serve:
- Fold the sides of the tortilla over the filling and then roll from the bottom to create a wrap.

Serve Warm:
- Serve the Spinach and Feta Breakfast Wraps immediately while they are warm.

These wraps are not only great for breakfast but can also be enjoyed for brunch, lunch, or a quick and healthy dinner. Feel free to get creative with the ingredients and adjust the toppings based on your preferences.

Cinnamon Roll Waffles

Ingredients:

For the Cinnamon Roll Waffle Batter:

- 1 can (8-count) refrigerated cinnamon rolls with icing

For the Cinnamon Sugar Filling:

- 1/4 cup unsalted butter, melted
- 1/3 cup brown sugar, packed
- 1 teaspoon ground cinnamon

For the Cream Cheese Glaze:

- Reserved icing from the cinnamon roll can
- 2 tablespoons cream cheese, softened
- 1/2 cup powdered sugar
- 1/2 teaspoon vanilla extract

Instructions:

Preheat Waffle Iron:
- Preheat your waffle iron according to the manufacturer's instructions.

Separate Cinnamon Rolls:
- Separate the cinnamon rolls from the can, and set the icing aside.

Roll Out Dough:

- On a lightly floured surface, roll out each cinnamon roll into a flat, thin circle.

Prepare Cinnamon Sugar Filling:

- In a small bowl, mix together melted butter, brown sugar, and ground cinnamon to create the filling.

Spread Filling on Dough:

- Spread a thin layer of the cinnamon sugar filling over each rolled-out cinnamon roll.

Roll Up Cinnamon Rolls:

- Roll up each cinnamon roll tightly, similar to how you would roll cinnamon rolls.

Cook in Waffle Iron:

- Place each rolled cinnamon roll in the preheated waffle iron and cook according to the manufacturer's instructions until they are golden brown and cooked through.

Prepare Cream Cheese Glaze:

- While the waffles are cooking, prepare the cream cheese glaze. In a bowl, combine the reserved icing from the cinnamon roll can, softened cream cheese, powdered sugar, and vanilla extract. Mix until smooth.

Drizzle with Glaze:

- Once the waffles are cooked, remove them from the waffle iron and drizzle the cream cheese glaze over the top.

Serve and Enjoy:

- Serve the Cinnamon Roll Waffles warm and enjoy this delicious and indulgent breakfast treat.

These waffles capture the flavors of traditional cinnamon rolls but with a fun and unique twist. They're perfect for a special weekend breakfast or brunch. Feel free to customize with additional toppings like chopped nuts or a sprinkle of extra cinnamon.

Sausage and Mushroom Strata

Ingredients:

- 8 slices of day-old bread (such as French or Italian bread), cubed
- 1 pound (450g) sausage (pork or turkey), cooked and crumbled
- 1 cup mushrooms, sliced
- 1 cup shredded cheese (cheddar, mozzarella, or your favorite cheese)
- 6 large eggs
- 2 cups milk
- 1 teaspoon Dijon mustard
- 1/2 teaspoon salt
- 1/4 teaspoon black pepper
- 1/4 cup fresh parsley, chopped (optional)
- Cooking spray or butter for greasing the baking dish

Instructions:

Prepare the Ingredients:
- Preheat the oven to 350°F (175°C). Grease a 9x13-inch baking dish with cooking spray or butter.

Layer the Bread and Sausage:
- Place half of the bread cubes in the prepared baking dish. Sprinkle half of the cooked and crumbled sausage over the bread.

Add Mushrooms and Cheese:
- Scatter half of the sliced mushrooms and half of the shredded cheese over the sausage layer.

Repeat Layers:
- Repeat the layers with the remaining bread, sausage, mushrooms, and cheese.

Prepare the Egg Mixture:
- In a mixing bowl, whisk together the eggs, milk, Dijon mustard, salt, and black pepper until well combined.

Pour Egg Mixture Over Layers:
- Pour the egg mixture evenly over the layered ingredients in the baking dish. Press down on the layers with a spatula to ensure the bread absorbs the liquid.

Optional: Add Fresh Parsley:
- Sprinkle chopped fresh parsley over the top if desired.

Cover and Refrigerate (Optional):
- At this point, you can cover the baking dish with plastic wrap and refrigerate for at least 2 hours or overnight. This allows the flavors to meld and the bread to absorb the egg mixture.

Bake:
- When ready to bake, remove the dish from the refrigerator and let it come to room temperature for about 30 minutes. Preheat the oven to 350°F (175°C) if not already preheated.
- Bake the strata for 45-50 minutes or until the top is golden brown and the center is set.

Cool and Serve:
- Allow the strata to cool for a few minutes before slicing. Serve warm.

Sausage and Mushroom Strata is a versatile dish that can be prepared ahead, making it perfect for entertaining or a stress-free weekend brunch. Enjoy the layers of savory goodness in every bite!

Lemon Ricotta Pancakes

Ingredients:

- 1 cup all-purpose flour
- 1 tablespoon sugar
- 1 teaspoon baking powder
- 1/2 teaspoon baking soda
- 1/4 teaspoon salt
- 1 cup ricotta cheese
- 3/4 cup milk
- 2 large eggs
- Zest of 1 lemon
- Juice of 1 lemon
- 1 teaspoon vanilla extract
- Butter or oil for cooking

Instructions:

Prepare Dry Ingredients:

- In a large bowl, whisk together the flour, sugar, baking powder, baking soda, and salt.

Prepare Wet Ingredients:

- In a separate bowl, combine the ricotta cheese, milk, eggs, lemon zest, lemon juice, and vanilla extract. Mix until well combined.

Combine Wet and Dry Ingredients:

- Pour the wet ingredients into the bowl with the dry ingredients. Gently fold the mixture until just combined. Do not overmix; it's okay if there are a few lumps.

Preheat Griddle or Pan:

- Preheat a griddle or a non-stick skillet over medium heat. Add a small amount of butter or oil to grease the surface.

Cook the Pancakes:

- Scoop 1/4 cup portions of batter onto the griddle for each pancake. Cook until bubbles form on the surface and the edges look set.

Flip and Cook:

- Flip the pancakes and cook for an additional 1-2 minutes on the other side, or until golden brown.

Repeat:

- Repeat the process with the remaining batter, adding more butter or oil to the griddle as needed.

Serve Warm:

- Serve the Lemon Ricotta Pancakes warm with your favorite toppings. Suggestions include fresh berries, maple syrup, powdered sugar, or a dollop of whipped cream.

Optional Garnish:

- Garnish with additional lemon zest for a burst of citrus flavor.

Lemon Ricotta Pancakes are light, fluffy, and have a wonderful combination of tartness from the lemon and creaminess from the ricotta. They make a perfect weekend breakfast or brunch treat!

Vegetarian Breakfast Burritos

Ingredients:

For the Burrito Filling:

- 1 tablespoon olive oil
- 1 small onion, diced
- 1 bell pepper, diced (any color)
- 1 small zucchini, diced
- 1 cup black beans, cooked and drained
- 1 cup corn kernels (fresh, frozen, or canned)
- 1 teaspoon ground cumin
- 1/2 teaspoon chili powder
- Salt and black pepper, to taste
- Optional: 1/2 cup diced tomatoes or salsa

For the Burritos:

- Large flour tortillas
- Scrambled eggs (4-6 eggs, depending on the number of burritos)
- Shredded cheese (cheddar, Monterey Jack, or your choice)
- Fresh cilantro, chopped (optional)
- Avocado slices or guacamole
- Sour cream or Greek yogurt (optional)
- Hot sauce or salsa (optional)

Instructions:

Prepare the Burrito Filling:

- In a skillet, heat olive oil over medium heat. Add diced onion and cook until softened.

Cook Vegetables:

- Add diced bell pepper and zucchini to the skillet. Cook until the vegetables are tender, about 5-7 minutes.

Add Black Beans and Corn:

- Stir in black beans and corn. Add ground cumin, chili powder, salt, and black pepper. Cook for an additional 2-3 minutes. If using diced tomatoes or salsa, add them at this stage.

Prepare Scrambled Eggs:

- In a separate pan, scramble the eggs until just cooked through.

Assemble the Burritos:

- Warm the tortillas in a dry skillet or microwave to make them pliable.
- On each tortilla, layer the scrambled eggs, vegetable mixture, shredded cheese, and chopped cilantro.

Add Avocado or Guacamole:

- Place avocado slices or a spoonful of guacamole on top.

Optional Toppings:

- Add any additional toppings you like, such as sour cream, Greek yogurt, hot sauce, or more salsa.

Fold and Roll:

- Fold the sides of the tortilla over the filling, then roll from the bottom to create a burrito.

Serve Warm:

- Place the burritos seam-side down on a plate to hold them together. Serve warm.

Vegetarian Breakfast Burritos are versatile, and you can customize them with your favorite vegetables, cheeses, and toppings. They are perfect for a hearty breakfast or a portable brunch option. Enjoy!

Breakfast Pizza

Ingredients:

For the Pizza Dough:

- 1 pound pizza dough (store-bought or homemade)
- Flour (for dusting)

For the Toppings:

- 1 tablespoon olive oil
- 1 cup shredded mozzarella cheese
- 4 large eggs
- Salt and black pepper, to taste
- 4 slices cooked bacon, crumbled
- 1/2 cup diced bell peppers (any color)
- 1/2 cup diced tomatoes
- Chopped fresh chives or parsley (for garnish)

Instructions:

Preheat the Oven:
- Preheat your oven to the temperature specified on the pizza dough package or recipe instructions.

Prepare Pizza Dough:
- If using store-bought pizza dough, let it come to room temperature if it was refrigerated. Dust a work surface with flour and roll out the pizza dough to your desired thickness.

Transfer to Pizza Stone or Pan:
- Transfer the rolled-out dough to a pizza stone or a baking sheet.

Prebake the Dough (Optional):
- Prebaking the dough for a few minutes can help ensure a crispy crust. Bake according to the dough instructions or until the edges are just starting to turn golden.

Add Olive Oil and Cheese:
- Brush the pizza dough with olive oil. Sprinkle shredded mozzarella cheese evenly over the dough.

Crack Eggs on Pizza:
- Carefully crack the eggs onto the pizza, spreading them out evenly.

Season with Salt and Pepper:
- Sprinkle salt and black pepper over the eggs to taste.

Add Toppings:
- Scatter crumbled bacon, diced bell peppers, and diced tomatoes over the pizza.

Bake:
- Bake in the preheated oven according to the pizza dough instructions or until the crust is golden, and the eggs are cooked to your liking. Keep an eye on the eggs to prevent overcooking the yolks.

Garnish and Serve:
- Once out of the oven, sprinkle chopped fresh chives or parsley over the top. Slice and serve immediately.

Optional: Drizzle with Hot Sauce or Sriracha (Optional):
- If you like some heat, you can drizzle hot sauce or sriracha over the breakfast pizza before serving.

Enjoy your Breakfast Pizza as a delightful and savory start to the day! Feel free to customize it with your favorite breakfast ingredients and toppings.

Caprese Avocado Toast

Ingredients:

- 2 slices whole-grain bread (or your preferred bread)
- 1 ripe avocado
- 1 large tomato, sliced
- Fresh mozzarella cheese, sliced
- Fresh basil leaves
- Balsamic glaze (store-bought or homemade)
- Extra virgin olive oil
- Salt and pepper, to taste

Instructions:

Toast the Bread:
- Toast the slices of bread to your desired level of crispiness.

Prepare the Avocado:
- While the bread is toasting, peel and pit the avocado. Mash the avocado in a bowl with a fork and season with salt and pepper to taste.

Assemble the Toast:
- Spread the mashed avocado evenly over each slice of toasted bread.

Layer with Tomato Slices:
- Place tomato slices on top of the mashed avocado.

Add Mozzarella:
- Arrange slices of fresh mozzarella over the tomatoes.

Top with Basil Leaves:

- Scatter fresh basil leaves over the mozzarella. Basil adds a wonderful aromatic and herbal flavor.

Drizzle with Balsamic Glaze:

- Drizzle balsamic glaze over the top of the toast. If you don't have balsamic glaze, you can use a balsamic reduction or even regular balsamic vinegar.

Finish with Olive Oil:

- Drizzle extra virgin olive oil over the toast for added richness and flavor.

Season and Serve:

- Season the Caprese Avocado Toast with a pinch of salt and pepper if needed.

Enjoy Immediately:

- Serve the Caprese Avocado Toast immediately while the bread is still warm.

This Caprese Avocado Toast is a delightful combination of creamy avocado, juicy tomatoes, fresh mozzarella, and aromatic basil. It's a perfect way to elevate your avocado toast game with the flavors of a classic Caprese salad. Enjoy it as a delicious and satisfying breakfast or snack!

Sweet Potato Hash

Ingredients:

- 2 medium-sized sweet potatoes, peeled and diced into small cubes
- 1 onion, finely chopped
- 1 bell pepper, diced (any color)
- 2 tablespoons olive oil or cooking oil of your choice
- 1 teaspoon smoked paprika
- 1/2 teaspoon ground cumin
- 1/2 teaspoon garlic powder
- Salt and black pepper, to taste
- Optional: 1/4 teaspoon cayenne pepper for some heat
- Fresh parsley or green onions, chopped (for garnish)
- Eggs (optional, for serving on top)

Instructions:

Prepare the Sweet Potatoes:
- Peel and dice the sweet potatoes into small, even cubes.

Sauté Onion and Bell Pepper:
- Heat olive oil in a large skillet over medium heat. Add chopped onion and bell pepper. Sauté until the vegetables are softened and the onion is translucent.

Add Sweet Potatoes:
- Add the diced sweet potatoes to the skillet. Spread them out into an even layer.

Season with Spices:

- Sprinkle smoked paprika, ground cumin, garlic powder, salt, black pepper, and cayenne pepper (if using) over the sweet potatoes. Stir to coat the sweet potatoes evenly with the spices.

Cook until Golden Brown:

- Allow the sweet potatoes to cook without stirring for a few minutes to develop a golden brown crust. Then, stir and let them cook again, repeating until the sweet potatoes are tender and crispy on the edges. This usually takes about 15-20 minutes.

Adjust Seasoning:

- Taste and adjust the seasoning as needed. Add more salt, pepper, or spices according to your preference.

Garnish:

- Garnish the sweet potato hash with chopped fresh parsley or green onions for a burst of freshness.

Serve:

- Serve the Sweet Potato Hash on its own as a side dish or as a base for other toppings. It pairs well with fried or poached eggs for a complete and satisfying breakfast.

Sweet Potato Hash is not only delicious but also versatile. You can customize it by adding ingredients like diced ham, crumbled bacon, or spinach. Enjoy this hearty and nutritious dish for a tasty meal any time of the day!

Pesto and Tomato Bruschetta

Ingredients:

- Baguette or Italian bread, sliced
- 2 cups cherry tomatoes, diced
- 1/4 cup fresh basil leaves, thinly sliced
- 2 tablespoons pesto sauce (store-bought or homemade)
- 1 clove garlic, peeled and halved
- Extra virgin olive oil
- Balsamic glaze (optional)
- Salt and black pepper, to taste

Instructions:

Preheat the Oven:
- Preheat your oven to 375°F (190°C).

Slice and Toast the Bread:
- Arrange the bread slices on a baking sheet. Toast in the preheated oven for about 5-7 minutes or until they are golden and crispy.

Prepare Tomatoes and Basil:
- In a bowl, combine diced cherry tomatoes and thinly sliced fresh basil. Season with salt and black pepper to taste.

Add Pesto Sauce:
- Add the pesto sauce to the tomato and basil mixture. Stir until well combined.

Rub Garlic on Toasted Bread:

- Take the toasted bread slices and rub each one with the halved garlic clove. This imparts a subtle garlic flavor to the bread.

Assemble the Bruschetta:

- Spoon the pesto and tomato mixture generously onto each garlic-rubbed bread slice.

Drizzle with Olive Oil:

- Drizzle extra virgin olive oil over the top of each bruschetta.

Optional: Balsamic Glaze:

- Optionally, drizzle balsamic glaze over the bruschetta for an extra layer of flavor.

Serve Immediately:

- Serve the Pesto and Tomato Bruschetta immediately while the bread is still warm and crispy.

Enjoy:

- Enjoy this vibrant and delicious appetizer as a delightful starter or snack.

Pesto and Tomato Bruschetta is a crowd-pleaser and a perfect way to celebrate the flavors of summer. The combination of fresh tomatoes, basil, and pesto creates a burst of freshness with every bite. Serve it at gatherings, parties, or as a light appetizer before a meal.

Chia Seed Pudding

Ingredients:

- 1/4 cup chia seeds
- 1 cup milk (dairy or plant-based, such as almond, coconut, or soy)
- 1-2 tablespoons maple syrup or honey (adjust to taste)
- 1 teaspoon vanilla extract

Instructions:

Combine Ingredients:

- In a bowl or jar, combine chia seeds, milk, maple syrup or honey, and vanilla extract.

Whisk Well:

- Whisk the mixture thoroughly to ensure the chia seeds are evenly distributed and don't clump together.

Let it Rest:

- Let the mixture rest for a few minutes and then whisk again to break up any clumps.

Refrigerate:

- Cover the bowl or jar and refrigerate the chia seed pudding for at least 2 hours, or ideally overnight. This allows the chia seeds to absorb the liquid and create a pudding-like consistency.

Stir Before Serving:

- Before serving, give the pudding a good stir to make sure it's well-mixed and has a smooth texture.

Customize:

- You can customize your chia seed pudding by adding various toppings and flavors. Some popular additions include fresh fruit (berries, mango, banana slices), nuts, seeds, granola, or a drizzle of nut butter.

Flavor Variations:

- Chocolate Chia Pudding:
    - Add 1-2 tablespoons of cocoa powder or chocolate chips to the basic recipe.
- Fruit-infused Pudding:
    - Blend fruits like berries, mango, or banana and mix them into the pudding for a fruity flavor.
- Matcha Chia Pudding:
    - Add 1 teaspoon of matcha powder for a delicious matcha-flavored pudding.
- Spiced Chia Pudding:
    - Add a pinch of cinnamon, nutmeg, or cardamom for a warm and spiced twist.

Experiment with different flavors and find your favorite combination. Chia seed pudding is not only tasty but also a good source of omega-3 fatty acids, fiber, and protein. Enjoy it as a guilt-free treat or a healthy breakfast option!

Ham and Cheese Croissants

Ingredients:

- 4 large croissants
- 8 slices ham (choose your favorite type)
- 4 slices Swiss or Gruyère cheese
- Dijon mustard (optional, for spreading)
- 1 tablespoon unsalted butter, melted (for brushing)

Instructions:

Preheat the Oven:
- Preheat your oven to 350°F (175°C).

Slice Croissants:
- Carefully slice each croissant horizontally, creating a top and bottom half.

Spread Dijon Mustard (Optional):
- If desired, spread a thin layer of Dijon mustard on the bottom half of each croissant.

Layer Ham and Cheese:
- Place a slice of ham and a slice of cheese on the bottom half of each croissant.

Assemble Croissants:
- Place the top half of the croissants over the ham and cheese to assemble the sandwiches.

Brush with Melted Butter:

- Brush the top of each croissant with melted butter. This adds a golden and crispy finish to the croissants.

Bake:

- Place the assembled croissants on a baking sheet and bake in the preheated oven for about 8-10 minutes, or until the cheese is melted, and the croissants are heated through.

Serve Warm:

- Remove the ham and cheese croissants from the oven and serve them warm.

These Ham and Cheese Croissants are simple to make and incredibly tasty. They are a perfect choice for a quick and satisfying breakfast or brunch. You can also add extra ingredients like sliced tomatoes, lettuce, or even a fried egg for additional flavor and variety. Enjoy!

Coconut Pancakes

Ingredients:

- 1 cup all-purpose flour
- 2 tablespoons sugar
- 1 teaspoon baking powder
- 1/2 teaspoon baking soda
- 1/4 teaspoon salt
- 3/4 cup coconut milk
- 1/4 cup plain yogurt
- 1 large egg
- 2 tablespoons melted coconut oil
- 1/2 teaspoon vanilla extract
- 1/3 cup shredded coconut (sweetened or unsweetened)
- Butter or oil for cooking

Instructions:

Mix Dry Ingredients:

- In a bowl, whisk together the flour, sugar, baking powder, baking soda, and salt.

Prepare Wet Ingredients:

- In another bowl, whisk together the coconut milk, yogurt, egg, melted coconut oil, and vanilla extract.

Combine Wet and Dry Ingredients:

- Pour the wet ingredients into the dry ingredients and stir until just combined. Be careful not to overmix; a few lumps are okay.

Add Shredded Coconut:

- Gently fold in the shredded coconut into the pancake batter.

Preheat Griddle or Pan:

- Preheat a griddle or a non-stick skillet over medium heat. Add a small amount of butter or oil to grease the surface.

Cook Pancakes:

- Pour 1/4 cup portions of batter onto the griddle for each pancake. Cook until bubbles form on the surface and the edges look set.

Flip and Cook:

- Flip the pancakes and cook for an additional 1-2 minutes on the other side, or until golden brown.

Repeat:

- Repeat the process with the remaining batter, adding more butter or oil to the griddle as needed.

Serve Warm:

- Serve the Coconut Pancakes warm, topped with your favorite syrup, fresh fruit, or additional shredded coconut.

These Coconut Pancakes are light, fluffy, and have a wonderful coconut flavor. They are perfect for a tropical-inspired breakfast or brunch. Customize them to your liking by adding chopped nuts or a drizzle of chocolate or caramel sauce. Enjoy!

Egg and Bacon Breakfast Quesadillas

Ingredients:

- 4 large flour tortillas
- 4 large eggs
- 4 slices bacon, cooked and crumbled
- 1 cup shredded cheddar cheese (or your favorite cheese)
- 1/2 cup diced bell peppers (any color)
- 1/4 cup diced red onion
- Salt and black pepper, to taste
- Cooking spray or butter for greasing the skillet
- Optional toppings: salsa, sour cream, avocado slices, chopped cilantro

Instructions:

Cook Bacon:

- Cook the bacon slices until crispy. Remove from the pan, let them cool, and then crumble them.

Prepare Egg Scramble:

- In a bowl, whisk the eggs and season with salt and black pepper. Cook the eggs in the same skillet used for the bacon, stirring occasionally until soft scrambled.

Assemble Quesadillas:

- Lay out the tortillas and distribute the scrambled eggs evenly over half of each tortilla.

Add Bacon and Vegetables:

- Sprinkle crumbled bacon, shredded cheddar cheese, diced bell peppers, and diced red onion over the scrambled eggs.

Fold and Cook:

- Fold the other half of the tortilla over the filling to create a half-moon shape. Press down gently.

Cook in Skillet:

- Heat a skillet or griddle over medium heat and lightly grease with cooking spray or butter. Cook each quesadilla for 2-3 minutes per side, or until the tortilla is golden brown and the cheese is melted.

Slice and Serve:

- Remove the quesadillas from the skillet, let them rest for a moment, and then slice each one into wedges.

Serve with Toppings:

- Serve the Egg and Bacon Breakfast Quesadillas warm with optional toppings like salsa, sour cream, avocado slices, or chopped cilantro.

These quesadillas are versatile, and you can customize them with your favorite ingredients. Feel free to add other veggies, different types of cheese, or even a dash of hot sauce for extra flavor. Enjoy your delicious and hearty breakfast!

Chocolate Banana Bread

Ingredients:

- 3 ripe bananas, mashed
- 1/2 cup unsalted butter, melted
- 1 teaspoon vanilla extract
- 2 large eggs
- 1 cup granulated sugar
- 1 1/2 cups all-purpose flour
- 1/2 cup unsweetened cocoa powder
- 1 teaspoon baking soda
- 1/4 teaspoon salt
- 1 cup chocolate chips or chunks (optional)
- Chopped nuts (walnuts or pecans), optional for added crunch

Instructions:

Preheat the Oven:
- Preheat your oven to 350°F (175°C). Grease a 9x5-inch loaf pan.

Mash Bananas:
- In a large mixing bowl, mash the ripe bananas with a fork or potato masher.

Add Wet Ingredients:
- Add melted butter, vanilla extract, and eggs to the mashed bananas. Mix well.

Add Sugar:

- Stir in the granulated sugar until the mixture is well combined.

Combine Dry Ingredients:

- In a separate bowl, whisk together the flour, cocoa powder, baking soda, and salt.

Mix Wet and Dry Ingredients:

- Gradually add the dry ingredients to the banana mixture, mixing until just combined. Do not overmix.

Add Chocolate Chips and Nuts:

- If using, fold in the chocolate chips or chunks and chopped nuts until evenly distributed in the batter.

Transfer to Loaf Pan:

- Pour the batter into the greased loaf pan, spreading it evenly.

Bake:

- Bake in the preheated oven for about 55-65 minutes, or until a toothpick inserted into the center comes out clean or with a few moist crumbs. The baking time may vary, so start checking around 50 minutes.

Cool:

- Allow the chocolate banana bread to cool in the pan for about 10 minutes, then transfer it to a wire rack to cool completely.

Slice and Serve:

- Once cooled, slice the chocolate banana bread and serve. Enjoy it as is or with a dollop of whipped cream or a scoop of vanilla ice cream.

This Chocolate Banana Bread is moist, rich, and perfect for satisfying your chocolate cravings. It's a great way to use up ripe bananas and create a delicious treat for breakfast or dessert.

Prosciutto-Wrapped Asparagus

Ingredients:

- Fresh asparagus spears, woody ends trimmed
- Thinly sliced prosciutto
- Olive oil
- Black pepper, to taste

Instructions:

Preheat the Oven:

- Preheat your oven to 400°F (200°C).

Prepare the Asparagus:

- Wash and trim the woody ends from the asparagus spears. If the asparagus is thick, you can peel the lower part of the stalks for better texture.

Wrap Asparagus with Prosciutto:

- Take a slice of prosciutto and wrap it around each asparagus spear. You can wrap it tightly or leave some parts exposed for a decorative look.

Place on Baking Sheet:

- Place the prosciutto-wrapped asparagus spears on a baking sheet lined with parchment paper or aluminum foil.

Drizzle with Olive Oil:

- Drizzle the wrapped asparagus with a bit of olive oil. This adds flavor and helps crisp up the prosciutto.

Season with Black Pepper:

- Grind some black pepper over the asparagus for added flavor.

Bake:

- Bake in the preheated oven for about 12-15 minutes or until the asparagus is tender, and the prosciutto becomes crispy.

Serve Warm:

- Remove from the oven and serve the prosciutto-wrapped asparagus warm.

Optional: Balsamic Reduction Drizzle (Optional):

- If desired, you can drizzle a balsamic reduction over the prosciutto-wrapped asparagus for extra flavor.

Serve as an Appetizer or Side Dish:

- Prosciutto-wrapped asparagus is perfect as an appetizer for a gathering or as a side dish for a special meal.

This simple yet flavorful dish brings together the savory taste of prosciutto and the freshness of asparagus. It's quick to prepare and adds a touch of sophistication to any occasion. Enjoy!

Ricotta and Berry Stuffed Crepes

Ingredients:

For the Crepes:

- 1 cup all-purpose flour
- 2 large eggs
- 1 cup milk
- 1/4 cup water
- 2 tablespoons melted butter
- 1 tablespoon sugar
- 1/4 teaspoon salt
- Additional butter for cooking

For the Filling:

- 1 cup ricotta cheese
- 2 tablespoons powdered sugar (adjust to taste)
- 1 teaspoon vanilla extract

For the Berry Compote:

- 1 cup mixed berries (strawberries, blueberries, raspberries)
- 2 tablespoons sugar
- 1 tablespoon water
- 1 teaspoon lemon juice

Instructions:

Prepare Crepe Batter:

- In a blender, combine flour, eggs, milk, water, melted butter, sugar, and salt. Blend until the batter is smooth. Let the batter rest for about 15-30 minutes.

Cook Crepes:

- Heat a non-stick skillet or crepe pan over medium heat. Add a small amount of butter to coat the pan.
- Pour a small amount of batter into the center of the pan, swirling it to spread the batter thinly and evenly.
- Cook for about 1-2 minutes on each side until the crepe is lightly golden. Repeat with the remaining batter. Stack cooked crepes on a plate, covering them with a kitchen towel to keep warm.

Prepare Ricotta Filling:

- In a bowl, mix ricotta cheese, powdered sugar, and vanilla extract until well combined. Adjust the sweetness to your liking.

Make Berry Compote:

- In a small saucepan, combine mixed berries, sugar, water, and lemon juice. Simmer over medium heat until the berries break down and the mixture thickens slightly. Remove from heat and let it cool.

Assemble Crepes:

- Place a spoonful of the ricotta filling on one side of each crepe and fold it in half, then fold it again to form a triangle.

Serve with Berry Compote:

- Drizzle the stuffed crepes with the berry compote. You can also dust them with powdered sugar for an extra touch.

Optional: Garnish:

- Garnish with additional fresh berries and mint leaves if desired.

Ricotta and Berry Stuffed Crepes are a delightful combination of creamy ricotta, sweet berries, and delicate crepes. They make for a beautiful presentation and are perfect for a special breakfast or dessert. Enjoy!

Breakfast Tacos

Ingredients:

- Soft corn or flour tortillas
- Eggs (scrambled, fried, or your preferred style)
- Breakfast protein of choice (e.g., cooked bacon, sausage, chorizo, or vegetarian alternatives)
- Shredded cheese (cheddar, Monterey Jack, or your favorite cheese)
- Salsa or pico de gallo
- Avocado slices or guacamole
- Chopped fresh cilantro
- Sour cream or Greek yogurt (optional)
- Lime wedges for serving

Instructions:

Cook Breakfast Protein:
- Cook your choice of breakfast protein (bacon, sausage, chorizo, etc.) according to the package instructions or your preferred method. Set aside.

Prepare Eggs:
- Cook the eggs in your preferred style (scrambled, fried, or even as an omelette). Season with salt and pepper to taste.

Warm Tortillas:
- Heat the tortillas in a dry skillet or microwave them according to the package instructions until warm and pliable.

Assemble Tacos:

- Lay out the warmed tortillas. Add a portion of the cooked eggs to each tortilla.

Add Breakfast Protein:
- Top the eggs with your cooked breakfast protein of choice.

Sprinkle Cheese:
- Sprinkle shredded cheese over the eggs and protein. The warmth from the eggs and protein will melt the cheese.

Add Fresh Toppings:
- Layer on fresh toppings such as salsa or pico de gallo, avocado slices or guacamole, and chopped cilantro.

Optional Toppings:
- Add a dollop of sour cream or Greek yogurt if desired.

Squeeze Lime:
- Squeeze fresh lime juice over the tacos for a burst of citrus flavor.

Fold and Serve:
- Fold the tacos and serve them warm. You can use a taco holder or simply fold them in half.

Feel free to get creative and add additional toppings like sliced jalapeños, diced tomatoes, or a hot sauce of your choice. Breakfast tacos are versatile and easily customizable to suit your taste preferences. Enjoy this delicious and satisfying breakfast option!

Sourdough Breakfast Sandwich

Ingredients:

- 1 large sourdough English muffin or a slice of sourdough bread
- 1 large egg
- 1 slice of cheese (cheddar, Swiss, or your preference)
- 2 slices of cooked bacon or breakfast sausage patty
- Salt and pepper to taste
- Butter or cooking spray for cooking
- Optional toppings: avocado slices, tomato, spinach, hot sauce

Instructions:

Prepare the Sourdough Bread:

- If using an English muffin, slice it in half. If using a slice of sourdough bread, toast it lightly.

Cook the Egg:

- In a skillet over medium heat, melt a small amount of butter or use cooking spray. Crack the egg into the skillet and cook to your preference (fried, scrambled, or as an omelette). Season with salt and pepper.

Add Cheese:

- Place a slice of cheese on top of the cooking egg and let it melt.

Assemble the Sandwich:

- If you cooked a fried egg, place it on the bottom half of the sourdough English muffin or bread. If you made scrambled eggs or an omelette, you can fold it to fit the sandwich.

Add Bacon or Sausage:

- Layer the cooked bacon or breakfast sausage patty on top of the egg and cheese.

Optional Toppings:

- Add any optional toppings you desire, such as avocado slices, tomato, spinach, or a drizzle of hot sauce.

Top with the Other Half:

- Place the other half of the sourdough English muffin or bread on top to complete the sandwich.

Serve Warm:

- Serve the sourdough breakfast sandwich warm and enjoy!

Feel free to customize the sandwich based on your preferences. You can experiment with different cheeses, add veggies, or use a different type of breakfast meat. The tangy flavor of sourdough adds a unique twist to the classic breakfast sandwich.

Carmelized Onion and Goat Cheese Frittata

Ingredients:

- 8 large eggs
- 1/4 cup milk or cream
- Salt and pepper to taste
- 2 tablespoons olive oil
- 2 large onions, thinly sliced
- 1 tablespoon balsamic vinegar (optional)
- 4 ounces goat cheese, crumbled
- Fresh herbs (such as thyme or chives) for garnish

Instructions:

Preheat the Oven:

- Preheat your oven to 375°F (190°C).

Caramelize Onions:

- In an oven-safe skillet, heat olive oil over medium heat. Add the thinly sliced onions and cook, stirring occasionally, until they become golden brown and caramelized. This process may take about 15-20 minutes. If desired, you can add a tablespoon of balsamic vinegar to enhance the flavor during the last few minutes of cooking.

Whisk Eggs:

- In a bowl, whisk together the eggs, milk or cream, salt, and pepper until well combined.

Add Eggs to Onions:

- Pour the whisked eggs over the caramelized onions in the skillet. Allow the eggs to set around the edges.

Add Goat Cheese:

- Sprinkle crumbled goat cheese evenly over the frittata.

Bake in the Oven:

- Transfer the skillet to the preheated oven and bake for about 15-20 minutes or until the frittata is set in the center and the top is lightly golden.

Garnish and Serve:

- Once the frittata is cooked, remove it from the oven. Garnish with fresh herbs, such as thyme or chives.

Slice and Serve:

- Allow the frittata to cool for a few minutes, then slice it into wedges. Serve warm.

This Caramelized Onion and Goat Cheese Frittata is rich, savory, and has a wonderful combination of sweet caramelized onions and tangy goat cheese. It's a versatile dish that you can enjoy for various occasions. Serve it on its own, with a side salad, or as part of a brunch spread. Enjoy!

Peaches and Cream Stuffed French Toast

Ingredients:

For the Stuffed French Toast:

- 8 slices of thick-cut bread (such as brioche or challah)
- 4 ounces cream cheese, softened
- 1/2 cup peach preserves or fresh diced peaches
- 4 large eggs
- 1 cup milk
- 1 teaspoon vanilla extract
- 1/2 teaspoon ground cinnamon
- Pinch of salt
- Butter for cooking

For Serving:

- Fresh peach slices
- Maple syrup
- Powdered sugar (optional)

Instructions:

Prepare the Filling:
- In a bowl, mix the softened cream cheese with peach preserves or diced peaches until well combined.

Make the Sandwiches:

- Spread the cream cheese and peach mixture onto four slices of bread, and top with the remaining slices to make sandwiches.

Whisk the Egg Mixture:

- In a shallow dish, whisk together the eggs, milk, vanilla extract, ground cinnamon, and a pinch of salt.

Dip and Coat:

- Dip each stuffed sandwich into the egg mixture, ensuring both sides are coated evenly.

Cook on a Griddle or Skillet:

- Heat a griddle or skillet over medium heat and melt a bit of butter. Cook each stuffed French toast sandwich until golden brown on both sides.

Serve:

- Place the cooked stuffed French toast on a plate. Top with fresh peach slices, drizzle with maple syrup, and sprinkle with powdered sugar if desired.

Enjoy:

- Serve the Peaches and Cream Stuffed French Toast warm and enjoy the delicious combination of creamy filling and sweet peaches.

This Peaches and Cream Stuffed French Toast is a perfect blend of flavors and textures, making it a delightful breakfast or brunch treat. It's a great way to enjoy the sweetness of ripe peaches in a comforting and satisfying dish.

Bacon and Egg Breakfast Pies

Ingredients:

- 1 package refrigerated pie crusts (or homemade if preferred)
- 6 slices of bacon, cooked and crumbled
- 6 large eggs
- 1/2 cup shredded cheddar cheese
- Salt and pepper to taste
- Chopped chives or parsley for garnish (optional)

Instructions:

Preheat the Oven:
- Preheat your oven according to the instructions on the pie crust package or to around 375°F (190°C).

Prepare the Pie Crusts:
- Roll out the pie crusts and use a round cutter or a bowl to cut circles that fit into a standard muffin tin. Press the circles into the muffin tin to form crusts.

Cook Bacon:
- Cook the bacon until crispy, then crumble it into small pieces.

Pre-Bake Pie Crusts:
- Pre-bake the pie crusts for a few minutes according to the package instructions or until they are just starting to set.

Add Bacon to Crusts:
- Sprinkle a portion of the crumbled bacon into each pre-baked pie crust.

Crack Eggs into Each Pie:

- Carefully crack one egg into each pie crust, ensuring not to break the yolk. Season with salt and pepper to taste.

Top with Cheese:

- Sprinkle shredded cheddar cheese over the eggs in each pie.

Bake:

- Place the muffin tin in the preheated oven and bake for about 15-20 minutes or until the egg whites are set, and the yolks are still slightly runny.

Garnish and Serve:

- Remove the Bacon and Egg Breakfast Pies from the oven, garnish with chopped chives or parsley if desired, and serve warm.

These individual breakfast pies are a convenient way to enjoy a classic bacon and egg combination. The pie crust provides a flaky and buttery base for the eggs and bacon, creating a delicious handheld breakfast. Feel free to customize by adding additional ingredients such as diced vegetables, herbs, or different types of cheese. Enjoy!

Tea:

Classic Black Tea

Ingredients:

- Black tea leaves (loose or in tea bags)
- Fresh water

Instructions:

Choose Your Tea:

- Select your favorite black tea. Common varieties include Assam, Darjeeling, Earl Grey, English Breakfast, and Ceylon.

Measure the Tea:

- If using loose tea leaves, measure about 1 teaspoon of leaves per 8 ounces of water. Adjust according to your taste preference.

Boil Fresh Water:

- Use fresh, cold water. Bring it to a rolling boil. Water quality is crucial for a good cup of tea, so use filtered or bottled water if your tap water doesn't taste good on its own.

Preheat the Teapot or Teacup:

- Pour a small amount of boiling water into the teapot or teacup, swirl it around, and then discard the water. This helps to warm the vessel and enhances the flavor of the tea.

Add Tea Leaves:

- Place the measured tea leaves directly into the teapot or a tea infuser if you're using loose tea. If using tea bags, place one bag in the teapot or teacup.

Pour Boiling Water:

- Pour the boiling water over the tea leaves or tea bag. Use about 8 ounces of water for each cup.

Steep the Tea:

- Let the tea steep for 3 to 5 minutes. Adjust the steeping time based on your preference for a stronger or milder flavor.

Remove Tea Leaves or Tea Bag:

- Once steeped, remove the tea leaves or tea bag to prevent over-steeping, which can make the tea bitter.

Optional Additions:

- Add sugar, honey, milk, or lemon if desired. Black tea is versatile and can be enjoyed in various ways.

Enjoy:

- Sip and savor your classic black tea. Enjoy it plain or with your preferred additions.

Black tea is known for its bold and brisk flavor, making it a perfect choice for breakfast or afternoon tea. Experiment with different varieties and find the one that suits your taste preferences. Whether enjoyed hot or cold, black tea is a timeless and comforting beverage.

Green Tea with Mint

Ingredients:

- Green tea leaves (loose or in tea bags)
- Fresh mint leaves (about 5-6 leaves per cup)
- Fresh water
- Optional: Honey or sweetener of choice, lemon slices

Instructions:

Choose Your Green Tea:

- Select your preferred green tea. Common varieties include Sencha, Dragon Well (Longjing), Gunpowder, or Jasmine green tea.

Measure the Tea:

- If using loose tea leaves, measure about 1 teaspoon of leaves per 8 ounces of water. Adjust based on your taste preference.

Boil Fresh Water:

- Use fresh, cold water. Bring it to a temperature of around 175°F to 185°F (80°C to 85°C). Avoid using boiling water for green tea to prevent bitterness.

Preheat the Teapot or Teacup:

- Preheat your teapot or teacup by pouring a small amount of hot water into it. Swirl the water around, then discard it. This helps to warm the vessel.

Add Green Tea Leaves:

- Place the measured green tea leaves directly into the teapot or a tea infuser if using loose tea. If using tea bags, place one bag in the teapot or teacup.

Pour Hot Water:

- Pour the hot water over the green tea leaves. Use about 8 ounces of water for each cup.

Steep the Tea:

- Let the green tea steep for 2 to 3 minutes. Green tea generally requires a shorter steeping time compared to black tea.

Add Fresh Mint Leaves:

- While the tea is steeping, bruise the fresh mint leaves by gently pressing them between your fingers to release their oils. Add the mint leaves to the teapot or teacup.

Continue Steeping:

- Allow the green tea and mint to steep together for an additional 1 to 2 minutes. Adjust the steeping time based on your desired mint flavor intensity.

Strain or Remove Tea Leaves:

- If using loose tea leaves, strain the tea to remove them. If using tea bags, you can remove the bag.

Optional Additions:

- Add honey or sweetener of choice to taste. You can also add a slice of lemon for a citrusy twist.

Enjoy:

- Sip and enjoy your refreshing Green Tea with Mint. It's perfect for a moment of relaxation or as a pick-me-up.

Green tea with mint is not only delicious but also provides the health benefits associated with green tea and the soothing properties of mint. Adjust the ingredients and steeping time to suit your preferences and create your perfect cup.

Chai Latte

Ingredients:

- 1 cup water
- 1 black tea bag or 1 tablespoon loose black tea leaves
- 1/2 cup milk (whole milk, almond milk, soy milk, or your preference)
- 1-2 tablespoons sweetener (sugar, honey, or maple syrup)
- 1/2 teaspoon ground cinnamon
- 1/4 teaspoon ground ginger
- 1/4 teaspoon ground cardamom
- 1/8 teaspoon ground cloves
- 1/8 teaspoon ground nutmeg
- Optional: a dash of black pepper for a bit of heat
- Optional: whipped cream or cinnamon for garnish

Instructions:

Prepare the Chai Spice Blend:

- In a small bowl, mix together the ground cinnamon, ground ginger, ground cardamom, ground cloves, and ground nutmeg. Set aside.

Brew the Black Tea:

- In a saucepan, bring the water to a boil. Add the black tea bag or loose tea leaves and steep for 3 to 5 minutes, depending on your desired strength.

Add Chai Spice Blend:

- While the tea is steeping, add 1 teaspoon of the chai spice blend to the water. Adjust the amount based on your taste preference.

Sweeten the Tea:

- Stir in the sweetener of your choice, adjusting the amount to your preferred level of sweetness.

Froth or Heat the Milk:

- In a separate saucepan or using a milk frother, heat the milk until it's hot but not boiling. If you have a frother, you can also froth the milk for a creamier texture.

Combine Tea and Milk:

- Pour the spiced tea into a cup. Slowly add the hot, frothed milk over the tea.

Optional Garnishes:

- Top with whipped cream or a sprinkle of cinnamon if desired.

Serve and Enjoy:

- Stir the Chai Latte gently and enjoy the comforting blend of spiced tea and creamy milk.

Feel free to customize the Chai Latte to suit your taste. You can adjust the spice levels, experiment with different types of milk, and vary the sweetener according to your preference. Making Chai Lattes at home allows you to create a warm and flavorful beverage tailored to your liking.

Iced Lemon Tea

Ingredients:

- 4 to 6 black tea bags (or your preferred tea variety)
- 4 cups water
- 1/2 cup freshly squeezed lemon juice (about 2-3 lemons)
- 1/2 cup granulated sugar (adjust to taste)
- Ice cubes
- Lemon slices for garnish (optional)
- Fresh mint leaves for garnish (optional)

Instructions:

Brew the Tea:
- Boil 4 cups of water. Place the tea bags in a heatproof pitcher, and pour the boiling water over the tea bags. Let it steep for about 5 minutes or according to the tea package instructions.

Add Sweetener:
- While the tea is still hot, stir in the granulated sugar. Adjust the sweetness according to your preference. Stir until the sugar is completely dissolved.

Cool the Tea:
- Allow the tea to cool to room temperature. You can let it sit on the counter or place it in the refrigerator for faster cooling.

Add Lemon Juice:
- Once the tea has cooled, add freshly squeezed lemon juice to the pitcher. Stir well to combine.

Refrigerate:
- Place the pitcher in the refrigerator to chill the tea further. This will also help the flavors meld.

Serve Over Ice:
- When ready to serve, fill glasses with ice cubes. Pour the chilled lemon tea over the ice.

Garnish (Optional):
- Garnish the glasses with lemon slices and fresh mint leaves if desired.

Enjoy:
- Stir and enjoy your refreshing Iced Lemon Tea on a hot day or as a delightful beverage anytime.

Feel free to experiment with the level of sweetness and lemon flavor to suit your taste. You can also try adding a splash of sparkling water for some effervescence. Iced Lemon Tea is a versatile and simple drink that you can easily customize to create your perfect summer refreshment.

Earl Grey Tea Latte

Ingredients:

- 1 Earl Grey tea bag (or 1-2 teaspoons of loose Earl Grey tea)
- 1 cup water
- 1/2 cup milk (whole milk, almond milk, soy milk, or your preference)
- 1-2 tablespoons sweetener (sugar, honey, or vanilla syrup)
- Optional: a dash of vanilla extract
- Optional: lavender syrup for a traditional London Fog flavor
- Optional: whipped cream for topping

Instructions:

Brew the Earl Grey Tea:

- Boil 1 cup of water. Place the Earl Grey tea bag in a teapot or directly into a mug. Pour the boiling water over the tea bag and let it steep for about 3 to 5 minutes.

Add Sweetener and Optional Flavorings:

- Remove the tea bag and stir in the sweetener of your choice. If desired, add a dash of vanilla extract or a splash of lavender syrup for a traditional London Fog flavor.

Froth the Milk:

- In a separate saucepan or using a milk frother, heat the milk until it's hot but not boiling. Froth the milk until it becomes creamy and has a light foam.

Combine Tea and Frothed Milk:

- Pour the steeped and sweetened Earl Grey tea into a cup. Slowly add the frothed milk over the tea.

Optional Toppings:

- Top the Earl Grey Tea Latte with whipped cream if desired.

Serve and Enjoy:

- Stir the Earl Grey Tea Latte gently and enjoy the aromatic blend of tea, steamed milk, and sweetener.

The Earl Grey Tea Latte is known for its soothing and aromatic qualities, making it a perfect choice for a cozy beverage. You can customize the sweetness and flavorings to suit your taste preferences. Whether you prefer it classic or with a modern twist, the Earl Grey Tea Latte is a delightful treat.

Hibiscus Herbal Tea

Ingredients:

- 2 tablespoons dried hibiscus petals (or 2 hibiscus tea bags)
- 2 cups water
- Honey or sweetener of choice (optional)
- Lemon slices or mint leaves for garnish (optional)
- Ice cubes (for iced tea, optional)

Instructions:

Boil Water:
- Bring 2 cups of water to a boil in a pot or kettle.

Add Hibiscus Petals:
- Place the dried hibiscus petals in a heatproof pitcher or teapot. If using tea bags, add them directly to the pitcher.

Pour Boiling Water:
- Pour the boiling water over the hibiscus petals or tea bags.

Steep the Tea:
- Let the hibiscus steep for about 5 to 7 minutes. The longer you steep, the stronger the flavor. If you prefer a stronger tea, you can steep for up to 10 minutes.

Strain or Remove Tea Bags:
- If using loose petals, strain the tea to remove them. If using tea bags, you can simply remove them.

Sweeten (Optional):

- Add honey or your preferred sweetener to the tea, adjusting to your taste preference. Stir until the sweetener is fully dissolved.

Serve:
- Pour the hibiscus herbal tea into cups. You can serve it hot or over ice for a refreshing iced tea.

Garnish (Optional):
- Garnish with lemon slices or mint leaves for added freshness.

Enjoy:
- Sip and enjoy the vibrant and tangy flavor of hibiscus herbal tea.

Hibiscus herbal tea is known for its beautiful deep red color and its potential health benefits. It is rich in antioxidants and is often consumed for its potential to support heart health and lower blood pressure. Whether enjoyed hot or iced, hibiscus herbal tea is a delightful and visually appealing beverage.

Jasmine Pearl Tea

Ingredients:

- Jasmine Pearl Tea (1-2 teaspoons per 8 oz cup)
- Water (filtered or spring water is recommended)
- Optional: Jasmine blossoms for garnish
- Optional: Honey or sweetener of choice

Instructions:

Boil Water:

- Bring fresh, cold water to a boil. Let it cool slightly for a moment, as green tea benefits from slightly cooler water than boiling.

Preheat the Teapot or Teacup:

- Pour a small amount of hot water into the teapot or teacup to warm it. Swirl the water around, then discard it.

Add Jasmine Pearl Tea:

- Place 1-2 teaspoons of Jasmine Pearl Tea in the teapot or teacup. Adjust the quantity based on your preference and the size of your vessel.

Pour Hot Water:

- Pour the hot water over the Jasmine Pearl Tea leaves. Ensure that the water is around 175°F to 185°F (80°C to 85°C) to avoid scalding the delicate green tea leaves.

Steep the Tea:

- Let the tea steep for 2 to 3 minutes. Adjust the steeping time based on your preference for a lighter or stronger brew.

Strain the Tea:

- If you used loose Jasmine Pearl Tea, strain the tea into another teapot or directly into teacups to remove the tea leaves.

Optional Sweetening:

- If desired, add honey or sweetener of your choice to the tea. Stir until the sweetener is fully dissolved.

Garnish (Optional):

- Garnish with a few jasmine blossoms for a beautiful presentation and an extra touch of fragrance.

Enjoy:

- Sip and enjoy the exquisite aroma and delicate flavor of Jasmine Pearl Tea.

Jasmine Pearl Tea is a treat for the senses, with its floral aroma and gentle taste. It's best enjoyed on its own to appreciate the natural sweetness and complexity of the tea. Feel free to experiment with steeping times and tea-to-water ratios to find the balance that suits your taste.

Masala Chai

Ingredients:

- 2 cups water
- 1 cup milk (whole milk, almond milk, or your preference)
- 2-3 teaspoons loose black tea or 2-3 tea bags
- 2-3 teaspoons granulated sugar or sweetener of choice (adjust to taste)
- 1 cinnamon stick
- 3-4 whole green cardamom pods, lightly crushed
- 3-4 whole cloves
- 1-2 thin slices of fresh ginger
- Optional: a pinch of black pepper or star anise for added warmth and flavor

Instructions:

Prepare the Spices:

- In a mortar and pestle, lightly crush the cardamom pods, cloves, and ginger to release their flavors. You can also use the back of a spoon to crush them.

Boil Water:

- In a pot, bring 2 cups of water to a boil.

Add Spices and Tea:

- Add the crushed spices, cinnamon stick, and black tea to the boiling water. Let it simmer for about 5 minutes to allow the flavors to infuse.

Add Milk:

- Pour in the milk and continue simmering. Be careful not to let it boil over.

Sweeten:
- Add the sugar or sweetener of your choice. Adjust the sweetness according to your taste.

Simmer:
- Allow the Chai to simmer for an additional 5 minutes, ensuring that it is well-infused with the spices.

Strain:
- Once the Chai is ready, strain the liquid to remove the tea leaves and spices. You can use a fine mesh sieve or a tea strainer.

Serve:
- Pour the strained Masala Chai into cups. You can enjoy it plain or with a slice of lemon.

Optional: Froth the Chai (Chai Latte):
- If you like, use a milk frother to froth the Chai for a creamier texture.

Enjoy:
- Sip and enjoy the warm and flavorful Masala Chai.

Feel free to adjust the spice levels and sweetness to suit your taste preferences. Masala Chai is a versatile drink, and you can experiment with different spice combinations to create your perfect cup of spiced tea.

Peach Ginger White Tea

Ingredients:

- 2 teaspoons white tea leaves or 2 white tea bags
- 1 ripe peach, sliced (or 1 cup of frozen peach slices)
- 1 teaspoon fresh ginger, sliced or grated
- 2 cups water
- Honey or sweetener of choice (optional)
- Peach slices and fresh mint for garnish (optional)

Instructions:

Prepare White Tea:

- If using loose white tea leaves, place them in a teapot or infuser. If using tea bags, place them directly in a teapot or teacup.

Add Peach and Ginger:

- Add the sliced peach and fresh ginger to the teapot or infuser.

Boil Water:

- In a saucepan, bring 2 cups of water to a near-boil. Pour the hot water over the white tea leaves, peach slices, and ginger.

Steep the Tea:

- Let the tea steep for about 3 to 5 minutes. Adjust the steeping time based on your preference for a lighter or stronger brew.

Strain or Remove Tea Bags:

- If using loose tea leaves, strain the tea to remove them. If using tea bags, you can simply remove the bags.

Sweeten (Optional):

- Add honey or your preferred sweetener to the tea, stirring until it's fully dissolved. Adjust the sweetness according to your taste.

Garnish (Optional):

- Garnish with additional peach slices and fresh mint for a decorative touch.

Serve:

- Pour the Peach Ginger White Tea into cups and serve hot.

Enjoy:

- Sip and enjoy the delicate flavor of white tea combined with the sweetness of peach and the warmth of ginger.

This Peach Ginger White Tea is not only delicious but also packed with antioxidants. It can be served hot or over ice for a refreshing iced tea during warmer weather. Adjust the ingredients and sweetness to suit your taste preferences, and feel free to experiment with different tea-to-fruit ratios.

Mango Black Tea Punch

Ingredients:

- 4 cups brewed black tea (cooled)
- 1 cup mango puree (fresh or store-bought)
- 1/2 cup orange juice
- 1/4 cup lemon juice
- 1/4 cup simple syrup (adjust to taste)
- 1-2 cups cold water (adjust to desired strength)
- Ice cubes
- Fresh mango slices and mint leaves for garnish

Instructions:

Brew Black Tea:
- Brew 4 cups of black tea and allow it to cool to room temperature.

Prepare Mango Puree:
- Peel and dice a ripe mango. Blend the mango pieces until smooth to create mango puree. You can also use store-bought mango puree.

Make Simple Syrup:
- In a small saucepan, combine equal parts water and sugar. Heat over medium heat, stirring until the sugar dissolves. Allow the simple syrup to cool.

Mix Ingredients:
- In a large pitcher, combine the brewed black tea, mango puree, orange juice, lemon juice, and simple syrup. Stir well to combine.

Adjust Sweetness and Strength:

- Taste the punch and adjust the sweetness by adding more simple syrup if needed. You can also adjust the strength by adding cold water if the flavor is too concentrated.

Chill:

- Refrigerate the Mango Black Tea Punch until it's thoroughly chilled.

Serve:

- Fill glasses with ice cubes and pour the chilled Mango Black Tea Punch over the ice.

Garnish:

- Garnish each glass with fresh mango slices and mint leaves for a tropical touch.

Enjoy:

- Stir and enjoy the refreshing and fruity flavor of Mango Black Tea Punch.

This punch is perfect for warm days or as a party drink. It combines the richness of black tea with the sweet and vibrant notes of mango, creating a delightful and thirst-quenching beverage. Adjust the sweetness and fruitiness to suit your taste, and feel free to get creative with additional garnishes or a splash of sparkling water for some effervescence.

Turmeric Ginger Tea

Ingredients:

- 1 teaspoon ground turmeric (or 1 tablespoon fresh turmeric, grated)
- 1 teaspoon fresh ginger, grated
- 1-2 teaspoons honey or sweetener of choice (adjust to taste)
- 1-2 teaspoons lemon juice (optional)
- 2 cups water

Instructions:

Prepare Turmeric and Ginger:
- If using fresh turmeric and ginger, peel and grate them. If using ground turmeric, measure out the specified amount.

Boil Water:
- Bring 2 cups of water to a boil in a small saucepan.

Add Turmeric and Ginger:
- Add the grated turmeric and ginger to the boiling water.

Simmer:
- Reduce the heat to low and let the mixture simmer for about 10 minutes to allow the flavors to infuse.

Strain:
- After simmering, strain the tea to remove the turmeric and ginger pieces. You can use a fine mesh sieve or a tea strainer.

Sweeten and Add Lemon (Optional):

- Add honey or your preferred sweetener to the tea, adjusting to your taste. If you like, add lemon juice for a citrusy twist.

Stir:
- Stir the tea well to ensure that the sweetener is fully dissolved.

Serve:
- Pour the Turmeric Ginger Tea into cups and serve hot.

Enjoy:
- Sip and enjoy the soothing and warming qualities of Turmeric Ginger Tea.

Feel free to adjust the quantities of turmeric, ginger, honey, and lemon according to your taste preferences. Turmeric Ginger Tea is not only comforting but may also provide potential health benefits due to the anti-inflammatory properties of turmeric and ginger. It's a great beverage to enjoy during cold weather or as a comforting drink at any time.

Rose Milk Tea

Ingredients:

- 2 teaspoons black tea leaves or 2 black tea bags
- 1 cup water
- 1 cup milk (whole milk, almond milk, or your preference)
- 2-3 teaspoons rose syrup (adjust to taste)
- 1-2 teaspoons sugar or sweetener of choice (optional)
- Ice cubes (for iced rose milk tea)
- Dried rose petals for garnish (optional)

Instructions:

Brew Black Tea:

- In a saucepan, bring 1 cup of water to a boil. Add the black tea leaves or tea bags and let it steep for about 3 to 5 minutes.

Add Rose Syrup:

- Once the tea is brewed, add the rose syrup to the hot tea. Start with 2-3 teaspoons, and adjust according to your taste preference.

Sweeten (Optional):

- If desired, add sugar or sweetener of your choice to the tea. Stir until the sweetener is fully dissolved.

Heat Milk:

- In a separate saucepan, heat the milk until it's hot but not boiling.

Combine Tea and Milk:

- Pour the brewed rose tea into a cup. Slowly add the hot milk to the tea, stirring continuously.

Serve Hot or Over Ice:

- Rose Milk Tea can be served hot or poured over ice for a refreshing iced version. If making iced rose milk tea, let the hot tea cool before pouring it over ice.

Garnish (Optional):

- Garnish with dried rose petals for a decorative touch.

Enjoy:

- Sip and enjoy the delightful blend of black tea with the sweet and floral notes of rose.

Rose Milk Tea is a popular and aromatic beverage, especially in South Asian cuisine. The floral aroma of rose adds a unique and pleasant dimension to the classic black tea. Adjust the sweetness and rose syrup quantities to suit your taste preferences.

Matcha Latte

Ingredients:

- 1 teaspoon matcha powder
- 1-2 teaspoons sweetener of choice (e.g., honey, sugar, or maple syrup)
- 1 cup milk (whole milk, almond milk, soy milk, or your preference)
- Optional: Vanilla extract or flavored syrup for added sweetness and flavor
- Optional: Matcha whisk or a small whisk for mixing

Instructions:

Sift Matcha Powder:
- Sift the matcha powder into a bowl to remove any clumps and ensure a smooth consistency.

Add Sweetener:
- Add the sweetener of your choice to the matcha powder. Adjust the amount based on your preferred level of sweetness.

Mix Matcha and Sweetener:
- If you have a matcha whisk, use it to whisk the matcha powder and sweetener with a small amount of hot water (not boiling). Whisk until the mixture becomes smooth and frothy. If you don't have a matcha whisk, you can use a regular whisk or a fork.

Heat Milk:
- In a saucepan or using a milk frother, heat the milk until it's hot but not boiling.

Pour Matcha Mixture:

- Pour the matcha and sweetener mixture into a mug.

Add Hot Milk:

- Pour the hot milk over the matcha mixture.

Whisk and Froth:

- If you have a matcha whisk, you can use it to whisk the matcha and milk together, creating a frothy layer on top. If not, use a regular whisk or a fork to mix and create some froth.

Optional Flavoring:

- Add a drop of vanilla extract or your favorite flavored syrup for an extra layer of flavor.

Serve:

- Serve your Matcha Latte hot and enjoy the vibrant and comforting flavors.

Matcha Latte is not only delicious but also provides a boost of antioxidants and a gentle caffeine kick from the matcha. Feel free to customize the sweetness, milk type, and flavorings to suit your taste preferences.

Spiced Apple Chai

Ingredients:

- 2 cups water
- 2 black tea bags or 2 teaspoons loose black tea
- 1 cup apple juice or apple cider
- 1 cup milk (whole milk, almond milk, or your preference)
- 1-2 tablespoons brown sugar or sweetener of choice (adjust to taste)
- 1 cinnamon stick
- 3-4 whole cloves
- 3-4 green cardamom pods, lightly crushed
- 1-2 thin slices of fresh ginger
- Optional: a pinch of black pepper for warmth
- Optional: whipped cream for topping

Instructions:

Brew Black Tea:

- In a saucepan, bring 2 cups of water to a boil. Add the black tea bags or loose black tea and steep for 3 to 5 minutes.

Add Chai Spices:

- To the brewed tea, add the cinnamon stick, cloves, crushed cardamom pods, and ginger slices.

Simmer:

- Allow the tea and spices to simmer for about 5 minutes, allowing the flavors to meld.

Add Apple Juice:

- Pour in the apple juice or apple cider and stir well. Let it simmer for an additional 5 minutes.

Add Milk:

- Pour in the milk and continue simmering. Be careful not to let it boil over.

Sweeten:

- Add brown sugar or sweetener of your choice, adjusting to your preferred level of sweetness.

Strain:

- Once the Spiced Apple Chai is well-infused, strain the liquid to remove the tea leaves and spices. You can use a fine mesh sieve or a tea strainer.

Optional Whipped Cream:

- If desired, top each serving with a dollop of whipped cream for an indulgent touch.

Serve:

- Pour the Spiced Apple Chai into cups and serve hot.

Enjoy:

- Sip and enjoy the comforting and flavorful blend of chai spices and apple sweetness.

Spiced Apple Chai is perfect for the fall and winter seasons, bringing together the comforting flavors of chai and the seasonal delight of apples. Adjust the sweetness and spices according to your taste preferences.

Lavender Chamomile Tea

Ingredients:

- 2 teaspoons dried chamomile flowers or 1 chamomile tea bag
- 1 teaspoon dried lavender flowers or 1 lavender tea bag
- 2 cups hot water
- Honey or sweetener of choice (optional)
- Lemon slices for garnish (optional)

Instructions:

Prepare Chamomile and Lavender:
- If using loose chamomile and lavender flowers, place them in a teapot or an infuser. If using tea bags, place them directly in a teapot or teacup.

Boil Water:
- Bring 2 cups of water to a near-boil. The water should be hot but not boiling to preserve the delicate flavors of the herbs.

Pour Hot Water:
- Pour the hot water over the chamomile and lavender flowers.

Steep the Tea:
- Let the tea steep for about 5 minutes. Adjust the steeping time based on your preference for a lighter or stronger brew.

Strain or Remove Tea Bags:
- If using loose flowers, strain the tea to remove them. If using tea bags, you can simply remove them.

Sweeten (Optional):

- Add honey or your preferred sweetener to the tea, stirring until it's fully dissolved. Adjust the sweetness according to your taste.

Garnish (Optional):

- Garnish with lemon slices for a touch of citrusy freshness.

Serve:

- Pour the Lavender Chamomile Tea into cups and serve hot.

Enjoy:

- Sip and enjoy the gentle and calming flavors of lavender and chamomile.

Lavender Chamomile Tea is known for its relaxing properties and is often enjoyed before bedtime to promote a restful sleep. The combination of chamomile and lavender creates a fragrant and comforting herbal tea that is both soothing and delicious. Feel free to experiment with the herb-to-water ratio to achieve your preferred strength.

Pomegranate White Tea Spritzer

- Add honey or your preferred sweetener to the brewed white tea, stirring until it's fully dissolved. Adjust the sweetness according to your taste.

Chill:

- Place the sweetened white tea in the refrigerator to chill. You can also use ice cubes to speed up the cooling process.

Mix with Pomegranate Juice:

- Once the white tea is chilled, mix in the pomegranate juice.

Prepare Glasses:

- Fill glasses with ice cubes.

Pour Tea Mixture:

- Pour the chilled white tea and pomegranate juice mixture over the ice in each glass.

Top with Sparkling Water:

- Top each glass with sparkling water or club soda for a fizzy and refreshing kick. Pour it slowly to avoid excessive fizzing.

Garnish (Optional):

- Garnish with pomegranate arils and mint leaves for a decorative touch.

Stir Gently:

- Give the spritzer a gentle stir to mix the flavors.

Serve:

- Serve immediately and enjoy the Pomegranate White Tea Spritzer.

This spritzer is perfect for a hot day or as a non-alcoholic option for a social gathering. The combination of white tea and pomegranate provides a light and crisp flavor, while the addition of sparkling water adds effervescence. Adjust the sweetness and the ratio of tea to sparkling water to suit your taste preferences.

Cinnamon Orange Rooibos Tea

Ingredients:

- 2 rooibos tea bags or 2 teaspoons loose rooibos tea
- 1 cinnamon stick
- Peel of one orange (avoiding the bitter white pith)
- 2 cups hot water
- Honey or sweetener of choice (optional)
- Orange slices and cinnamon sticks for garnish (optional)

Instructions:

Prepare Rooibos Tea:
- Place the rooibos tea bags or loose tea in a teapot or infuser.

Add Cinnamon and Orange Peel:
- Break the cinnamon stick into a few pieces and add it to the tea. Add the peel of one orange, ensuring you only use the orange part and avoiding the bitter white pith.

Boil Water:
- Bring 2 cups of water to a near-boil. Pour the hot water over the rooibos tea, cinnamon, and orange peel.

Steep the Tea:
- Let the tea steep for about 5-7 minutes. Adjust the steeping time based on your preference for a lighter or stronger brew.

Strain or Remove Tea Bags:

- If using loose rooibos tea, strain the tea to remove the tea leaves and other ingredients. If using tea bags, you can simply remove them.

Sweeten (Optional):

- Add honey or your preferred sweetener to the tea, stirring until it's fully dissolved. Adjust the sweetness according to your taste.

Garnish (Optional):

- Garnish with orange slices and cinnamon sticks for a decorative touch.

Serve:

- Pour the Cinnamon Orange Rooibos Tea into cups and serve hot.

Enjoy:

- Sip and enjoy the warm and comforting blend of rooibos, cinnamon, and citrus.

This Cinnamon Orange Rooibos Tea is caffeine-free and has a naturally sweet and earthy flavor. The combination of cinnamon and orange adds a delightful twist to traditional rooibos tea. Adjust the ingredients and sweetness to suit your taste preferences.

Coconut Almond Chai

Ingredients:

- 2 black tea bags or 2 teaspoons loose black tea
- 1 cup water
- 1 cup coconut milk (canned or carton)
- 1/4 cup almond milk
- 1-2 tablespoons sweetened condensed milk or sweetener of choice
- 1 cinnamon stick
- 3-4 whole cloves
- 3-4 green cardamom pods, lightly crushed
- 1-2 thin slices of fresh ginger
- 1/4 teaspoon almond extract
- Optional: Shredded coconut or crushed almonds for garnish

Instructions:

Brew Black Tea:

- Steep the black tea bags or loose tea in 1 cup of hot water for about 3-5 minutes. Strain or remove the tea bags.

Prepare Chai Spices:

- In the same pot, add the cinnamon stick, cloves, crushed cardamom pods, and ginger slices to the brewed black tea.

Add Coconut Milk and Almond Milk:

- Pour in the coconut milk and almond milk. Stir well to combine.

Simmer:

- Simmer the mixture over medium heat for about 5-7 minutes, allowing the spices to infuse into the coconut and almond milk.

Add Sweetener and Almond Extract:

- Stir in sweetened condensed milk or your preferred sweetener, adjusting to taste. Add almond extract and stir to incorporate.

Strain:

- Strain the Coconut Almond Chai to remove the tea leaves and spices. You can use a fine mesh sieve or a tea strainer.

Optional Garnish:

- Garnish with shredded coconut or crushed almonds for added texture and flavor.

Serve:

- Pour the Coconut Almond Chai into cups and serve hot.

Enjoy:

- Sip and enjoy the rich and comforting blend of chai spices, coconut, and almond.

This Coconut Almond Chai is a delightful treat that combines the warmth of traditional chai with the creaminess of coconut and the nuttiness of almonds. Adjust the sweetness and spices according to your taste preferences. It's a perfect beverage for cozy evenings or when you want to indulge in a unique and comforting chai experience.

Blueberry Mint Iced Tea

Ingredients:

- 2 black tea bags or 2 teaspoons loose black tea
- 1 cup fresh or frozen blueberries
- 1/4 cup fresh mint leaves
- 1/4 cup honey or sweetener of choice (adjust to taste)
- 4 cups hot water
- Ice cubes
- Fresh blueberries and mint leaves for garnish

Instructions:

Brew Black Tea:

- Steep the black tea bags or loose tea in 4 cups of hot water for about 3-5 minutes. Allow it to cool to room temperature.

Prepare Blueberry Mint Blend:

- In a blender, combine the fresh or frozen blueberries and fresh mint leaves. Blend until you get a smooth puree.

Strain Blueberry Mint Puree:

- Strain the blueberry mint puree using a fine mesh sieve or cheesecloth to remove the solids, leaving a smooth liquid.

Sweeten:

- In a large pitcher, combine the brewed black tea with the blueberry mint puree. Add honey or your preferred sweetener, adjusting to your taste. Stir until the sweetener is fully dissolved.

Chill:

- Place the pitcher in the refrigerator and let it chill for at least 1-2 hours to enhance the flavors.

Serve Over Ice:

- Fill glasses with ice cubes and pour the chilled Blueberry Mint Iced Tea over the ice.

Garnish:

- Garnish each glass with a few fresh blueberries and mint leaves for a visually appealing touch.

Stir and Enjoy:

- Give the iced tea a gentle stir, and enjoy the refreshing and fruity flavor of Blueberry Mint Iced Tea.

This Blueberry Mint Iced Tea is perfect for hot summer days or as a delightful beverage to accompany a light meal. The combination of blueberries and mint adds a burst of freshness and a hint of sweetness to traditional iced tea. Adjust the sweetness and the ratio of tea to blueberry mint puree to suit your taste preferences.

Ginger Turmeric Golden Milk Tea

Ingredients:

- 1 cup milk (dairy or plant-based, like almond or coconut milk)
- 1 teaspoon ground turmeric
- 1/2 teaspoon ground ginger (or 1 teaspoon fresh grated ginger)
- 1/4 teaspoon ground cinnamon
- 1 pinch black pepper (enhances turmeric absorption)
- 1-2 teaspoons honey or sweetener of choice (adjust to taste)
- 1/2 teaspoon coconut oil (optional, for added richness)
- Optional: A dash of vanilla extract for flavor
- Optional: Turmeric root slices or cinnamon sticks for garnish

Instructions:

Prepare Milk:

- In a small saucepan, heat the milk over medium heat. Be careful not to let it boil.

Add Turmeric, Ginger, and Spices:

- Once the milk is warm, add the ground turmeric, ground ginger (or grated ginger), ground cinnamon, and a pinch of black pepper. Stir well to combine.

Simmer:

- Simmer the mixture over low heat for about 5 minutes, allowing the flavors to infuse. Keep stirring to prevent the mixture from sticking to the bottom.

Sweeten and Add Extras:

- Add honey or your preferred sweetener, adjusting to your taste. If desired, add coconut oil for added richness and a dash of vanilla extract for extra flavor. Stir until everything is well mixed.

Strain (Optional):

- If you prefer a smoother texture, you can strain the Golden Milk using a fine mesh sieve or cheesecloth to remove any ginger or turmeric particles.

Serve:

- Pour the Ginger Turmeric Golden Milk into a cup.

Garnish (Optional):

- Garnish with turmeric root slices or a cinnamon stick for an elegant touch.

Enjoy:

- Sip and enjoy the warm and soothing qualities of Ginger Turmeric Golden Milk Tea.

Golden Milk is known for the potential anti-inflammatory and antioxidant properties of turmeric. The combination of spices, along with the warmth of ginger, creates a comforting and aromatic drink. Adjust the sweetness and spice levels to suit your taste preferences.

Chocolate Chai Latte

Ingredients:

- 2 chai tea bags or 2 teaspoons loose chai tea
- 1 cup water
- 1 cup milk (dairy or plant-based)
- 2 tablespoons cocoa powder
- 2 tablespoons sugar or sweetener of choice (adjust to taste)
- 1/4 teaspoon ground cinnamon
- 1/4 teaspoon ground ginger
- 1/8 teaspoon ground cardamom
- 1 pinch black pepper
- Whipped cream for topping (optional)
- Chocolate shavings or cocoa powder for garnish (optional)

Instructions:

Brew Chai Tea:
- Steep the chai tea bags or loose tea in 1 cup of hot water for about 5 minutes. Strain or remove the tea bags.

Prepare Spices and Cocoa:
- In a small bowl, mix together the cocoa powder, sugar, ground cinnamon, ground ginger, ground cardamom, and a pinch of black pepper.

Heat Milk:
- In a saucepan, heat the milk over medium heat until it's warm but not boiling.

Combine Chai and Cocoa Mixture:
- Add the brewed chai tea to the cocoa and spice mixture. Stir well to combine.

Add Warm Milk:
- Pour the warm milk into the chai and cocoa mixture. Whisk or stir until everything is well blended.

Heat and Froth:
- Heat the combined mixture over medium heat, stirring constantly until it's hot but not boiling. If you have a milk frother, you can use it to froth the mixture for a latte-like texture.

Serve:
- Pour the Chocolate Chai Latte into mugs.

Top with Whipped Cream (Optional):
- If desired, top each mug with a dollop of whipped cream.

Garnish (Optional):
- Garnish with chocolate shavings or a sprinkle of cocoa powder for an extra touch of chocolatey goodness.

Enjoy:
- Sip and enjoy the rich and decadent flavor of Chocolate Chai Latte.

This Chocolate Chai Latte is perfect for those who enjoy the combination of chocolate and warm spices. Adjust the sweetness and the intensity of spices to suit your taste preferences. It's a comforting and indulgent beverage, perfect for cozy evenings or as a treat for yourself.

Minty Moroccan Mint Tea

Ingredients:

- 2 teaspoons loose green tea leaves or 2 green tea bags
- 3-4 sprigs of fresh mint (about 10-15 leaves)
- 3-4 teaspoons sugar or sweetener of choice (adjust to taste)
- 3 cups hot water
- Optional: Fresh mint leaves for garnish

Instructions:

Brew Green Tea:
- In a teapot, add the green tea leaves or tea bags.

Add Fresh Mint:
- Tear or bruise the fresh mint leaves slightly to release their flavor and add them to the teapot.

Pour Hot Water:
- Bring 3 cups of water to a near-boil, and then pour it over the green tea and mint leaves.

Steep:
- Allow the tea to steep for about 3-5 minutes. Adjust the steeping time based on your preference for a lighter or stronger brew.

Sweeten:
- Stir in sugar or your preferred sweetener, adjusting to taste. Traditionally, Moroccan Mint Tea is sweetened, but you can adjust the sweetness according to your preference.

Strain:
- Strain the tea to remove the tea leaves and mint. You can use a fine mesh sieve or a tea strainer.

Serve:
- Pour the Minty Moroccan Mint Tea into cups or small glasses.

Garnish (Optional):
- Garnish with additional fresh mint leaves for a decorative touch.

Enjoy:
- Sip and enjoy the refreshing and minty flavor of Moroccan Mint Tea.

Moroccan Mint Tea is not just a beverage; it's a cultural tradition in Morocco, often served in small glasses with a lot of flair. It's commonly enjoyed throughout the day, and the preparation process is considered an art form. Adjust the sweetness and the amount of mint to suit your taste, and feel free to experiment with the presentation to capture the essence of Moroccan tea culture.

Lemon Lavender Black Tea

Ingredients:

- 2 black tea bags or 2 teaspoons loose black tea
- Peel of one lemon (avoiding the bitter white pith)
- 1 teaspoon dried culinary lavender buds (food-grade)
- 2 cups hot water
- Honey or sweetener of choice (optional)
- Lemon slices or lavender sprigs for garnish (optional)

Instructions:

Brew Black Tea:
- Steep the black tea bags or loose tea in 2 cups of hot water for about 3-5 minutes. Strain or remove the tea bags.

Add Lemon Peel and Lavender:
- While the tea is still hot, add the peel of one lemon and the dried lavender buds to the tea. Stir gently to infuse the flavors.

Steep Again:
- Let the tea steep for an additional 3-5 minutes to allow the lemon peel and lavender to impart their flavors.

Strain:
- Strain the tea to remove the lemon peel, lavender, and any tea leaves. You can use a fine mesh sieve or a tea strainer.

Sweeten (Optional):

- Add honey or your preferred sweetener to the tea, stirring until it's fully dissolved. Adjust the sweetness according to your taste.

Garnish (Optional):

- Garnish each cup with a slice of lemon or a sprig of fresh lavender for an extra touch.

Serve:

- Pour the Lemon Lavender Black Tea into cups and serve hot.

Enjoy:

- Sip and enjoy the harmonious blend of black tea with the citrusy zing of lemon and the aromatic hints of lavender.

This Lemon Lavender Black Tea is not only flavorful but also provides a delightful combination of citrus and floral notes. Adjust the sweetness and the amount of lavender according to your taste preferences. It's a perfect beverage for a relaxing afternoon or whenever you crave a soothing and aromatic cup of tea.

Cranberry Orange Spice Tea

Ingredients:

- 2 black tea bags or 2 teaspoons loose black tea
- 1/4 cup dried cranberries
- Peel of one orange (avoiding the bitter white pith)
- 1 cinnamon stick
- 3-4 whole cloves
- 2 cups hot water
- Honey or sweetener of choice (optional)
- Orange slices and cranberries for garnish (optional)

Instructions:

Brew Black Tea:

- Steep the black tea bags or loose tea in 2 cups of hot water for about 3-5 minutes. Strain or remove the tea bags.

Add Cranberries and Orange Peel:

- While the tea is still hot, add the dried cranberries and the peel of one orange to the tea.

Add Spices:

- Place the cinnamon stick and whole cloves into the tea. Stir gently to infuse the flavors.

Steep Again:

- Allow the tea to steep for an additional 3-5 minutes to let the cranberries, orange peel, and spices impart their flavors.

Strain:

- Strain the tea to remove the cranberries, orange peel, and spices. You can use a fine mesh sieve or a tea strainer.

Sweeten (Optional):

- Add honey or your preferred sweetener to the tea, stirring until it's fully dissolved. Adjust the sweetness according to your taste.

Garnish (Optional):

- Garnish each cup with orange slices and a few dried cranberries for a festive touch.

Serve:

- Pour the Cranberry Orange Spice Tea into cups and serve hot.

Enjoy:

- Sip and enjoy the vibrant blend of black tea with the tartness of cranberries, the citrusy notes of orange, and the warmth of spices.

Cranberry Orange Spice Tea is a wonderful choice for the fall and winter seasons, offering a comforting and aromatic experience. Adjust the sweetness and the amount of cranberries and spices based on your preferences. It's a perfect beverage to enjoy by the fireplace or to serve at holiday gatherings.

Vanilla Rooibos Latte

Ingredients:

- 2 rooibos tea bags or 2 teaspoons loose rooibos tea
- 1 cup water
- 1 cup milk (dairy or plant-based)
- 1-2 tablespoons honey or sweetener of choice (adjust to taste)
- 1 teaspoon vanilla extract
- Optional: Whipped cream or frothed milk for topping
- Optional: Vanilla bean or vanilla pod for garnish

Instructions:

Brew Rooibos Tea:

- Steep the rooibos tea bags or loose tea in 1 cup of hot water for about 5-7 minutes. Strain or remove the tea bags.

Heat Milk:

- In a separate saucepan, heat the milk over medium heat until it's warm but not boiling.

Combine Tea and Milk:

- Pour the brewed rooibos tea into a mug. Add the warm milk to the tea.

Sweeten:

- Stir in honey or your preferred sweetener, adjusting to taste.

Add Vanilla Extract:

- Add the vanilla extract to the tea and milk mixture. Stir well to incorporate.

Optional Frothing:

- If you have a milk frother, you can froth the milk for a latte-like texture. Alternatively, you can top the latte with whipped cream.

Serve:
- Pour the Vanilla Rooibos Latte into a mug.

Optional Garnish:
- Garnish with a vanilla bean or a vanilla pod for an extra touch of vanilla aroma.

Enjoy:
- Sip and enjoy the comforting and aromatic Vanilla Rooibos Latte.

This Vanilla Rooibos Latte is a caffeine-free alternative to traditional lattes, making it a great option for those who want a soothing and flavorful beverage without the effects of caffeine. Adjust the sweetness and the amount of vanilla extract to suit your taste preferences. It's a perfect drink for a cozy afternoon or as a bedtime treat.

Strawberry Basil Iced Tea

Ingredients:

- 2 black tea bags or 2 teaspoons loose black tea
- 1 cup fresh strawberries, hulled and sliced
- 1/4 cup fresh basil leaves
- 4 cups hot water
- 2-4 tablespoons honey or sweetener of choice (adjust to taste)
- Ice cubes
- Fresh strawberry slices and basil leaves for garnish

Instructions:

Brew Black Tea:

- Steep the black tea bags or loose tea in 4 cups of hot water for about 3-5 minutes. Allow it to cool to room temperature.

Muddle Strawberries and Basil:

- In a pitcher, muddle the fresh strawberries and basil leaves. This helps release their flavors.

Add Tea:

- Pour the cooled black tea into the pitcher with the muddled strawberries and basil.

Sweeten:

- Stir in honey or your preferred sweetener, adjusting to taste. Make sure the sweetener is fully dissolved.

Refrigerate:

- Place the pitcher in the refrigerator and let it chill for at least 1-2 hours to enhance the flavors.

Strain (Optional):

- If you prefer a smoother texture, you can strain the Strawberry Basil Iced Tea to remove the strawberry and basil bits. Use a fine mesh sieve or cheesecloth.

Serve Over Ice:

- Fill glasses with ice cubes and pour the chilled Strawberry Basil Iced Tea over the ice.

Garnish:

- Garnish each glass with fresh strawberry slices and a basil leaf for a visually appealing touch.

Stir and Enjoy:

- Give the iced tea a gentle stir and enjoy the refreshing and fruity flavor of Strawberry Basil Iced Tea.

This Strawberry Basil Iced Tea is perfect for warm days or as a delightful beverage to accompany a summer brunch. The combination of strawberries and basil adds a burst of freshness and a hint of sweetness to traditional iced tea. Adjust the sweetness and the ratio of tea to strawberries and basil to suit your taste preferences.

Chamomile Honey GInger Tea

Ingredients:

- 2 chamomile tea bags or 2 teaspoons loose chamomile flowers
- 1-inch piece of fresh ginger, sliced
- 1-2 tablespoons honey (adjust to taste)
- 4 cups hot water
- Lemon slices (optional, for garnish)
- Fresh mint leaves (optional, for garnish)

Instructions:

Brew Chamomile Tea:

- Steep the chamomile tea bags or loose chamomile flowers in 4 cups of hot water for about 5 minutes. Strain or remove the tea bags.

Add Ginger:

- Add the sliced fresh ginger to the brewed chamomile tea. This adds a warm and slightly spicy element to the tea.

Sweeten:

- Stir in honey, adjusting to your preferred level of sweetness. Make sure the honey is fully dissolved.

Steep Again:

- Allow the tea to steep for an additional 3-5 minutes to infuse the flavors of ginger and chamomile.

Strain (Optional):

- If you prefer a smoother texture, you can strain the tea to remove the chamomile flowers and ginger slices. Use a fine mesh sieve or a tea strainer.

Serve:

- Pour the Chamomile Honey Ginger Tea into cups.

Garnish (Optional):

- Garnish each cup with a slice of lemon and a few fresh mint leaves for a refreshing touch.

Stir and Enjoy:

- Give the tea a gentle stir and savor the soothing and comforting flavor of Chamomile Honey Ginger Tea.

This tea is perfect for winding down in the evening or whenever you need a moment of relaxation. The combination of chamomile, honey, and ginger creates a harmonious blend of flavors that can be both calming and invigorating. Adjust the sweetness and the amount of ginger according to your taste preferences.

Pumpkin Spice Chai

Ingredients:

- 2 chai tea bags or 2 teaspoons loose chai tea
- 1 cup water
- 1/2 cup milk (dairy or plant-based)
- 2 tablespoons canned pumpkin puree
- 2 tablespoons brown sugar or sweetener of choice (adjust to taste)
- 1/2 teaspoon pumpkin spice blend (or a mix of cinnamon, nutmeg, ginger, and cloves)
- 1/2 teaspoon vanilla extract
- Whipped cream for topping (optional)
- Cinnamon sticks or a sprinkle of pumpkin spice for garnish (optional)

Instructions:

Brew Chai Tea:
- Steep the chai tea bags or loose tea in 1 cup of hot water for about 3-5 minutes. Strain or remove the tea bags.

Heat Milk and Pumpkin Puree:
- In a saucepan, heat the milk over medium heat. Add the canned pumpkin puree and whisk until well combined.

Combine Chai and Pumpkin Milk:
- Pour the brewed chai tea into the saucepan with the pumpkin milk mixture. Stir well.

Sweeten:

- Add brown sugar or your preferred sweetener to the chai and pumpkin mixture, adjusting to taste. Stir until the sweetener is fully dissolved.

Add Pumpkin Spice and Vanilla:

- Stir in the pumpkin spice blend and vanilla extract, infusing the mixture with warm and seasonal flavors.

Simmer:

- Simmer the Pumpkin Spice Chai over low heat for a few minutes, allowing the flavors to meld.

Optional Frothing:

- If you have a milk frother, you can froth the chai for a latte-like texture.

Serve:

- Pour the Pumpkin Spice Chai into mugs.

Top with Whipped Cream (Optional):

- If desired, top each mug with a dollop of whipped cream.

Garnish (Optional):

- Garnish with cinnamon sticks or a sprinkle of pumpkin spice for a festive touch.

Enjoy:

- Sip and enjoy the cozy and comforting flavor of Pumpkin Spice Chai.

This Pumpkin Spice Chai is perfect for the fall season, offering a delicious blend of chai spices and pumpkin goodness. Adjust the sweetness and spices according to your taste preferences, and feel free to customize with your favorite toppings. It's a wonderful beverage to cozy up with on a chilly day.

Blackberry Sage Tea

Ingredients:

- 2 black tea bags or 2 teaspoons loose black tea
- 1 cup fresh blackberries
- 4-5 fresh sage leaves
- 2 tablespoons honey or sweetener of choice (adjust to taste)
- 4 cups hot water
- Lemon slices for garnish (optional)
- Fresh blackberries and sage leaves for garnish (optional)

Instructions:

Brew Black Tea:

- Steep the black tea bags or loose tea in 4 cups of hot water for about 3-5 minutes. Strain or remove the tea bags.

Muddle Blackberries and Sage:

- In a pitcher, muddle the fresh blackberries and sage leaves to release their flavors.

Add Tea:

- Pour the brewed black tea into the pitcher with the muddled blackberries and sage.

Sweeten:

- Stir in honey or your preferred sweetener, adjusting to taste. Ensure the sweetener is fully dissolved.

Steep Again:

- Allow the tea to steep for an additional 3-5 minutes to let the blackberries and sage infuse their flavors.

Strain (Optional):

- If you prefer a smoother texture, you can strain the tea to remove the blackberry and sage bits. Use a fine mesh sieve or cheesecloth.

Serve Over Ice:

- Fill glasses with ice cubes and pour the Blackberry Sage Tea over the ice.

Garnish (Optional):

- Garnish each glass with lemon slices, fresh blackberries, and sage leaves for a visually appealing touch.

Stir and Enjoy:

- Give the iced tea a gentle stir and enjoy the refreshing and fruity flavor of Blackberry Sage Tea.

This Blackberry Sage Tea is perfect for warm days or as a unique and flavorful beverage to accompany a summer meal. The combination of blackberries and sage offers a delightful contrast of sweetness and herbal earthiness. Adjust the sweetness and the ratio of tea to blackberries and sage based on your taste preferences.

Coconut Chai Iced Tea

Ingredients:

- 2 chai tea bags or 2 teaspoons loose chai tea
- 1 cup water
- 1 cup coconut milk (canned or carton)
- 2 tablespoons sweetened condensed coconut milk (optional, for extra sweetness)
- 1-2 tablespoons honey or sweetener of choice (adjust to taste)
- Ice cubes
- Shredded coconut for garnish (optional)
- Cinnamon sticks or star anise for garnish (optional)

Instructions:

Brew Chai Tea:
- Steep the chai tea bags or loose tea in 1 cup of hot water for about 5 minutes. Strain or remove the tea bags.

Prepare Coconut Chai Base:
- In a separate container, mix the coconut milk with sweetened condensed coconut milk (if using). Stir well to combine.

Combine Tea and Coconut Milk:
- Pour the brewed chai tea into a pitcher. Add the coconut milk mixture to the pitcher. Stir well to mix the flavors.

Sweeten:

- Stir in honey or your preferred sweetener, adjusting to taste. Ensure that the sweetener is fully dissolved.

Chill:

- Place the pitcher in the refrigerator and let it chill for at least 1-2 hours to enhance the flavors.

Serve Over Ice:

- Fill glasses with ice cubes and pour the Coconut Chai Iced Tea over the ice.

Garnish (Optional):

- Garnish each glass with shredded coconut, cinnamon sticks, or star anise for an extra touch.

Stir and Enjoy:

- Give the iced tea a gentle stir and enjoy the exotic and flavorful Coconut Chai Iced Tea.

This Coconut Chai Iced Tea is a delightful treat that combines the richness of chai spices with the tropical sweetness of coconut. Adjust the sweetness and the amount of coconut milk according to your taste preferences. It's a perfect beverage for hot days or whenever you crave a unique and refreshing iced tea experience.

Raspberry Rosehip Herbal Tea

Ingredients:

- 2 teaspoons dried rosehips
- 1/2 cup fresh or frozen raspberries
- 2 teaspoons hibiscus petals (optional, for added color and tartness)
- 4 cups hot water
- 1-2 tablespoons honey or sweetener of choice (adjust to taste)
- Lemon slices or fresh mint for garnish (optional)

Instructions:

Prepare Rosehip and Raspberry Mixture:

- In a teapot or heatproof container, combine the dried rosehips, raspberries, and hibiscus petals if using.

Pour Hot Water:

- Bring 4 cups of water to a near-boil, and then pour it over the rosehips and raspberry mixture.

Steep:

- Allow the tea to steep for about 5-7 minutes. Longer steeping time will result in a stronger flavor.

Mash Raspberries:

- Using a spoon, gently mash the raspberries against the side of the teapot or container to release their juices.

Sweeten:

- Stir in honey or your preferred sweetener, adjusting to taste. Ensure that the sweetener is fully dissolved.

Strain:

- Strain the tea to remove the rosehips, raspberries, and any tea particles. You can use a fine mesh sieve or a tea strainer.

Serve:

- Pour the Raspberry Rosehip Herbal Tea into cups.

Garnish (Optional):

- Garnish each cup with lemon slices or fresh mint leaves for a refreshing touch.

Enjoy:

- Sip and enjoy the fruity and floral flavors of Raspberry Rosehip Herbal Tea.

This herbal tea is not only delicious but also rich in vitamin C, thanks to the rosehips. Adjust the sweetness and the amount of raspberries based on your taste preferences. It's a lovely beverage to enjoy either hot or chilled, making it a versatile and flavorful option for any time of the day.